UNIT

Edexcel AS | 1

History

Pursuing Life and Liberty:
Equality in the USA 1945–68 (Option D5)

Robin Bunce and Laura Gallagher

Series Editor: Derrick Murphy

Philip Allan Updates, an imprint of Hodder Education, an Hachette UK Company, Market Place, Deddington, Oxfordshire OX15 0SE

Orders

Bookpoint Ltd, 130 Milton Park, Abingdon, Oxfordshire OX14 4SB
tel: 01235 827720
fax: 01235 400454
e-mail: uk.orders@bookpoint.co.uk
Lines are open 9.00 a.m.–5.00 p.m., Monday to Saturday, with a 24-hour message answering service. You can also order through the Philip Allan Updates website: www.philipallan.co.uk

© Philip Allan Updates 2008

ISBN 978-0-340-96569-6

First printed 2008
Impression number 5 4 3 2
Year 2013 2012 2011 2010 2009

This guide has been written specifically to support students preparing for the Edexcel AS History Unit 1 examination. The content has been neither approved nor endorsed by Edexcel and remains the sole responsibility of the authors.

Typeset by DC Graphic Design, Swanley Village, Kent
Printed by MPG Books, Bodmin

Hachette UK's policy is to use papers that are natural, renewable and recyclable products and made from wood grown in sustainable forests. The logging and manufacturing processes are expected to conform to the environmental regulations of the country of origin.

Contents

Introduction

■ ■ ■

Content Guidance

■ ■ ■

Questions and Answers

Introduction

Aims of the unit

Unit 1 is worth 25% of the A-level (50% of the AS). It requires knowledge of the topic and the ability to explain historical events and assess their significance in a wider context. There are no sources in the exam, so source skills are unnecessary.

Questions require you to provide clear information that directly answers the question. In addition, examiners are looking for detailed and precise supporting evidence and examples to demonstrate that your statements are accurate. These examples need to be linked clearly to your argument.

You will have 40 minutes to write an answer to each question in the examination. In this time it is difficult to address every issue of some relevance to the question. Therefore, examiners will award full marks for answers that deal adequately, and in detail, with most of the central issues.

Pursuing Life and Liberty: Equality in the USA 1945–68 is Topic D5 of Paper 6HI01/D, A World Divided: Communism and Democracy in the Twentieth Century. You need to be prepared for at least two topics from Option D and in the exam you will be required to answer questions relating to two different topics. This book deals exclusively with Topic D5.

The examination paper

The exam paper has seven topics, and you are required to answer questions on two of these topics. Each topic contains two questions and you can only choose one of these questions. The format of the topic questions in a typical examination paper is as follows:

6HI01/D — A World Divided: Communism and Democracy in the Twentieth Century

Answer TWO questions: ONE question on each of the TWO topics for which you have been prepared. You may only answer ONE question on each topic.

D5 — Pursuing Life and Liberty: Equality in the USA, 1945–68

EITHER

9. Why did. . .   (Total: 30 marks)

OR

10.   How far. . .   (Total: 30 marks)

Examinable skills

A total of 60 marks are available for Unit 1. Marks will be awarded for demonstrating the following skills:

- focusing on the requirements of the question, such as the topic, the period specified and the 'key concept'
- remembering, choosing and using historical knowledge
- analysing, explaining and reaching a judgement
- showing links between the key factors of your explanation

Focusing on the requirements of the question

Read the question carefully to ensure that you have noted the topic, the period and the key concept that is being addressed. One of the following concepts will be addressed by each question: causation, consequence, continuity, chance and significance.

In the following question:

Why did the Black Power movement emerge in the late 1960s?

the topic is *the Black Power movement*, the period is the *late 1960s* and the key concept is causation — *explaining why it emerged.*

Remembering, choosing and using historical knowledge

When you have established what the question requires, you must decide which aspects of your own knowledge are relevant. Examiners are looking for an answer that covers between four and six factors. Next you must arrange these factors in a logical order to create a plan for your answer.

Once your structure is in place, you must develop it using specific examples. Try to ensure that your examples are detailed. You should include relevant dates; names of people, places, institutions and events; statistics and appropriate technical vocabulary. Examiners will reward both range and depth of knowledge.

Analysing, explaining and reaching a judgement

Telling the story of an event will not score well. It is expected that your answer will be arranged thematically, addressing different factors in turn.

Your key factors and supporting examples must be explicitly linked back to the question: that is to say, you must show how these details relate to or illustrate the argument that you are making. It is good practice to make these links at the end of each paragraph. It is also important that your essay reaches a clear judgement.

Showing links between the key factors of your explanation

In order to achieve the highest marks, you must highlight links between the factors that you have selected. This could mean demonstrating the relative importance of the different factors, or showing how the factors were dependent on each other.

Level descriptors

Answers are normally marked according to the five levels listed in the table below.

Level	Marks	Description
1	1–6	• General points are correct but not focused on the question • Lacks supporting evidence Level 1 answers are simplistic, irrelevant or vague.
2	7–12	• General points are focused on the question • Some accurate and relevant supporting evidence Level 2 answers might tell the story without addressing the question or list the key points without backing them up with specific examples.
3	13–18	• General points focus on the question • Accurate support, but this may be either partly relevant, lacking in detail or both Level 3 answers attempt to focus on the question but have significant areas of weakness. For example, the focus on the question may drift, the answer may lack specific examples or parts of the essay may simply tell the story.
4	19–24	• General points clearly address the question and show understanding of the most important factors involved • Accurate, relevant and detailed support • Clear explanatory links to the question Level 4 answers clearly attempt to answer the question and demonstrate a detailed knowledge of the period studied.
5	25–30	• General points clearly address the question and show understanding of the most important factors involved • Accurate, relevant and detailed support • Clear explanatory links to the question • Some supported discussion of the relative importance of the factors mentioned Level 5 answers are thorough and detailed. They clearly engage with the question, providing a balanced and carefully reasoned argument that reaches a clear and supported judgement.

How to use this guide

First, make sure that you understand the layout of the examination paper, the pattern of the marks and the types of question asked, all of which are explained above. Study the outline of the content required, which is given in the Content Guidance section. Try to:

- master the vocabulary and concepts given there
- establish clearly the important individuals and institutions which shaped the events of these years
- assess the extent of change by 1968

The most important part of the guide is the Questions and Answers section, which provides five examples of the kinds of question that you will be asked. It is important to work through these, studying the two sets of sample answers provided and the examiner's comments. The first answer to each question is an A-grade response which, although not perfect, gives a good idea of what is required. The purpose of the second answer is to illustrate some of the common errors made by students.

Content Guidance

The specification for **Pursuing Life and Liberty: Equality in the USA, 1945–68** states that the course covers four fundamental topics:

- The social and economic position of black citizens in the USA in the 1940s and early 1950s: the nature and extent of discrimination and segregation; signs of change by 1955.
- Martin Luther King and peaceful protest.
- Black Power and the use of violence; the extent to which equality had been achieved by 1968.
- The changing economic and social environment of the 1960s: the position of other ethnic minorities.

This option focuses predominantly on the struggle on the part of black Americans for equal rights between the end of the Second World War and the death of Martin Luther King in 1968. Candidates must be aware of the economic and social position of African Americans in different parts of the USA in the period immediately following the Second World War as well as the ways in which this position altered as the period progressed. In addition, candidates should be aware of the changing attitudes to civil rights during the period, specifically on the part of groups such as black Americans, white Americans, and the federal and state governments.

It is also necessary to understand the movement from peaceful protest to the later more militant campaigns of the Black Power movement. You should be able to assess the significance of the Civil Rights Acts during this period and the extent to which civil rights had been achieved by 1968. Finally, you will have to be able to place these changes in their wider context, assessing the significance of the protest culture of the 1960s and issues relating to Hispanic and Native Americans.

This guide will consider each of these fundamental topics in turn. However, examiners may set questions which require knowledge from more than one of these areas. For example, a question could be set which requires you to compare the achievements of peaceful protest with those of Black Power.

Outline of topics

1945–55: signs of change

Differences between north and south
- Social differences
- Political differences
- Economic differences

The impact of the Second World War and the beginning of the Cold War

Harry S. Truman (1945–53)

Early NAACP campaigns
- Why did the early NAACP campaigns use legal methods to fight segregation?
- Education and the Brown case, 1950–55
- Why did the early NAACP campaigns focus on education?
- Achievements of the early NAACP campaigns

Signs of change by 1955

1955–68: Martin Luther King and peaceful protest

Martin Luther King's background and ideology

Peaceful protest
- The focus of the campaigns
- Evaluating the success of peaceful protest

Opposition to equal rights
- Presidential opposition
- Opposition in Congress
- Opposition from state authorities and local police
- Opposition from the Federal Bureau of Investigation
- White opposition

Martin Luther King: saint or sinner?

Legal changes and the role of federal government
- Dwight D. Eisenhower (1953–61)
- John F. Kennedy (1961–63)
- Lyndon B. Johnson (1963–69)
- Congress and the Supreme Court

1960–68: Black Power and the use of violence

Unity and divisions in the civil rights movement, 1960–66
- Working together
- Increasing divisions

- Explaining the rise of black militancy

The impact of the Vietnam War

Black Power
- The Black Power movement
- Self-determination
- Violence
- Social and economic change
- Achievements of Black Power

What had the black movement achieved by 1968?

Gains: 1945–68

Explaining these achievements

The limits of progress by 1968

Why was progress limited?

The 1960s: changing economic and social context

Economic and social context
- Prosperity
- The Great Society
- How did economic concerns affect the struggle for civil rights?
- Education
- Mass culture

Protest culture
- Student rebels
- Vietnam protest
- Women's liberation
- Counterculture and individual freedom

Other racial minorities
- Native Americans
- Hispanic Americans

1945–55: signs of change

Differences between north and south

The American Civil War (1861–65) divided the USA between the north and the south. This division was of great importance to African Americans, as the northern states fought for the nationwide abolition of slavery whereas the southern states fought to preserve slavery, which was crucial to the southern economy. Victory for the north resulted in the national abolition of slavery and the **emancipation** of black slaves. Nonetheless, racial prejudice continued, and there were substantial differences in the treatment of black people between the northern and the southern states. These can be analysed as social, political and economic differences.

Social differences

Racism was especially severe in the south, where 'Jim Crow' laws, enacted between 1887 and 1891, segregated housing, schools, transport and public amenities along racial lines. In 1896 the principle of these laws was challenged. Homer Plessy claimed that Jim Crow laws were unconstitutional as they contravened the **14th Amendment**, which guaranteed the citizenship of all Americans whatever their race. Nonetheless, the **Supreme Court** upheld the Jim Crow laws and the case (*Plessy* v *Ferguson*, 1896) established the principle that 'separate but equal' treatment was lawful. Consequently, it was ruled constitutional to provide different services for black and white Americans, as long as these services were deemed 'equal'. In practice, however, services were never equal, and in some cases, state governments spent as much as ten times more on services for white people.

Broadly speaking, legal segregation was not a feature of life in the northern states. Blacks living in northern cities such as New York, Detroit, Cleveland, Chicago and Philadelphia, which all had significant black populations, faced informal segregation. Indeed, black people in the northern states tended to live in urban ghettos. There were no laws that forced them to live in specific areas, but economic and social circumstances limited the opportunities of blacks in the north. As a result, black and white communities often developed quite separately.

Political differences

As *Plessy* v *Ferguson* demonstrates, there were black people who were willing to fight the status quo. In the late nineteenth and early twentieth centuries, campaigners such as Booker T. Washington, W. E. B. Dubois and Marcus Garvey gave voice, in different ways, to black discontent. The most radical voices came from northern states. Dubois — sometimes described as the creator of the first civil rights movement — founded the National Association for the Advancement of Colored People (NAACP), which sought to overturn segregation through the courts, whereas Garvey advocated that African Americans leave the USA and go 'back to Africa'. However, most black people were not engaged in political struggle.

Indeed, in the south the struggle was extremely dangerous, with violently racist groups such as the **Ku Klux Klan** (KKK) enjoying increased popular support and political influence in the 1920s. Black people in the south had little legal protection from the KKK, and lynching of African Americans who were perceived to have challenged white dominance was commonplace. It was also difficult for African Americans to participate in political activity in southern states due to the Jim Crow laws, which effectively disenfranchised black citizens. Southern states traditionally used a variety of tactics, such as **grandfather clauses** and **literacy tests**, to exclude black people from voting.

In the northern states there were only pockets of Klan activity. Additionally, it was much easier for black people to exercise their right to vote. Indeed, black voters in the northern states played an important part in the election of Franklin Delano Roosevelt in the 1944 presidential election, as well as the election of African American Adam Clayton Powell to the House of Representatives from New York's Harlem district in 1945. Both of these facts emphasise the growing power of black voters in the northern states.

Economic differences

On average, black Americans were also poorer than white Americans. In the south, this was often a result of limited employment opportunities, which, in turn, resulted from discrimination in education. For example, education was segregated even at university level. White universities refused to accept black students and black universities had poorer facilities and were unable to offer postgraduate programmes such as PhDs. Generally, schools for black Americans had a quarter of the budget of schools that educated white children. Southern blacks also suffered from technological changes which affected farming in the 1940s. Traditionally, cotton farming had employed many black workers. However, by 1944 the mechanical cotton picker had been introduced. The machine could do the work of 50 people and therefore created large-scale unemployment amongst black **sharecroppers** in the south.

For black workers in the north, conditions were also bad. However, the problems that black people faced were not legal in nature, and in this sense black workers in the north had some advantages over black workers in the south. On average, black Americans in the north were twice as likely to be unemployed as their white counterparts. Additionally, black workers could expect to be paid only half of the average wage of white workers. What is more, following the end of the Second World War, black workers were five times more likely to be sacked from armament companies than white workers. Nonetheless, the majority of black workers in the north were members of trade unions. This was because union membership had been legalised by the Wagner Act 1935 and because the Ku Klux Klan was significantly less active in the north and therefore did not intimidate northern black workers.

The impact of the Second World War and the beginning of the Cold War

In many ways, the Second World War was a catalyst for the development of the civil rights movement. At the front, black GIs had fought for their country and therefore considered themselves US citizens in the fullest sense. Moreover, GIs stationed in the

UK and France observed and experienced a greater degree of racial integration than they were used to in the USA. What is more, both soldiers and political leaders were struck by the contradiction of fighting Nazi racism overseas, whilst segregation remained an accepted and legally entrenched practice both at home and in the army.

The Second World War also affected non-combatants. First, the war effort encouraged southern black workers to migrate north to fill jobs vacated by white people now serving as soldiers. By 1945 it is estimated that around 5 million southern blacks had left the south in search of better wages and opportunities. Black citizens who migrated north were affected in two ways: they experienced a society with less formal segregation and they received higher wages in northern factories than they would have done had they remained in southern agriculture. All of this led to the establishment of the Congress for Racial Equality (CORE), founded in 1942 to campaign for increased civil rights. CORE pioneered the strategy of non-violent direct action, organising **sit-ins** at segregated restaurants, and demanding desegregation on interstate transport, with limited success.

Pressure for change increased during the early years of the **Cold War**. The USA wanted to be seen as fighting for freedom and justice against communist oppression. Clearly, the USA's ability to be the international standard bearer for liberty was compromised by the continued racial inequalities that characterised US culture. These considerations — as well as the political power that was exercised in the 1944 and 1945 elections by black voters in the north — put pressure on President Truman (1945–53) to use federal government power to address the concerns of black citizens.

Harry S. Truman (1945–53)

As a senator in the early 1940s, Truman publicly opposed lynching and declared himself a believer in the brotherhood of all men regardless of race. Once elected president, however, Truman was slow to move on civil rights issues. In 1946, Truman established a committee to investigate violence against African Americans. The committee's report, *To Secure These Rights* (1947), recommended anti-lynching legislation, desegregation of inter-state transport and the armed forces, and federal support for civil rights lawsuits, as well as founding the United States Commission on Civil Rights. Truman accepted the findings of the report and in 1948 issued Executive Order 9981 to end segregation in the armed forces and the civil service. He also endeavoured to open more public housing to African Americans. In doing this, Truman faced opposition from Congress, his own party and the top officials in the military. Nonetheless, Truman set a precedent for presidential concern with civil rights.

Truman's interest in civil rights was in part due to political necessity. Although Truman still used racist terminology in private, he was careful not to do this in public. Truman was aware that, in the north at least, the Democrats needed the black vote. What is more, Truman was a determined Cold Warrior who knew that the USA could never be presented as the 'land of the free' while overt racial discrimination continued unchallenged. However, political necessity cannot completely explain Truman's concern with civil rights. He may have gained two-thirds of the black vote in the 1948 presidential election, but his stance on civil rights alienated southern Democrats, who were traditionally the core of the Democrat vote. Fundamentally, Truman was motivated by a desire to modernise the USA. He believed that segregation was bad for the economy and left the USA 80 years behind the rest of the world.

Early NAACP campaigns

The National Association for the Advancement of Colored People (NAACP) was founded by a multi-racial group of campaigners in 1909. It was originally called the National Negro Committee, and its founders included Ida Wells-Barnett, W. E. B. Dubois, and William English. It was established in order to ensure that the rights (in the broadest sense) of all people were upheld, and to fight racial hatred and discrimination. In its early years, it publicly opposed the introduction of segregation into federal government offices, brought in by Woodrow Wilson. It also put pressure on the government to reject the appointment of Supreme Court justices who were in favour of segregation or ambivalent towards lynching.

During the Second World War membership of the NAACP increased substantially from 50,000 to 450,000. This indicates the increasing confidence of African Americans during this period. Between 1945 and 1960, the NAACP used legal methods to challenge segregation in the south. Typically, it would provide legal support for black citizens involved in court cases opposing segregation. The most prominent of the NAACP's legal team was Special Counsel Thurgood Marshall, who became the first African-American Supreme Court Justice in 1967. Nevertheless, from the late 1950s, members of the NAACP, often sanctioned by the leadership of the NAACP, became involved in, and even organised, non-violent direct action. For example, Rosa Parks and the leaders of the Greensboro sit-ins were all members of the NAACP.

Why did early NAACP campaigns use legal methods to fight segregation?

The NAACP used legal methods because its leaders recognised that segregation had legal foundations. *Plessy* v *Ferguson* provided the legal basis for formal racial segregation. Consequently, segregation could not be overturned until the law was changed. The NAACP's strategy was to argue that Jim Crow laws were unconstitutional. It appealed to the 14th and 15th Amendments to the US constitution, which granted citizenship to all people born or naturalised in the USA, and asserted that the right to vote could not be denied on the grounds of race.

In the decade following the Second World War, the Supreme Court was the branch of government that was most active in advancing civil rights. The Supreme Court was, and is, the USA's highest court of law. The nine Supreme Court Justices had final authority to interpret the Constitution. They had the power to rule laws made by the US Congress and state legislatures unconstitutional. The NAACP's goal was to persuade the Supreme Court that Jim Crow was unconstitutional and therefore to order the institutions of segregation to be dismantled.

The NAACP's approach represented a belief that it was possible to work within the US system for the advancement of civil rights. It also indicated the belief that a **de jure** end to Jim Crow was a necessary precondition for racial equality. This does not imply that the NAACP was unconcerned with informal, or **de facto**, changes. Rather it shows that the NAACP believed that permanent change could come about only through legal change by overturning *Plessy* v *Ferguson*.

Education and the Brown case, 1950–55

Throughout the early 1950s, the NAACP focused on education. Its first success was the 1950 case, *Sweatt* v *Painter*. As a result of the case, the Supreme Court ruled that black people must receive the same level of graduate education as white people.

More important still was the landmark Brown case of 1954–55. Oliver Brown argued that public education did not provide the same level of service for black and white citizens. Specifically, he claimed that it was inequitable for his daughter to be excluded from a whites-only school 5 blocks from his house, and forced to attend an all-black school 20 blocks away. As a result, the Supreme Court explicitly outlawed racial segregation in public education facilities for two reasons. First, the doctrine of 'separate but equal' (established in *Plessy* v *Ferguson*, 1896) could never truly provide an equal public education for black and white Americans. Secondly, the Supreme Court recognised that *Plessy* v *Ferguson* contravened the 14th Amendment.

However, crucially the court stopped short of drawing up a timetable for desegregation. Consequently, even though segregation was now illegal, it continued, with the vast majority of southern politicians pledging their support for continued segregation. Even the Brown II case of 1955 — ruling that desegregation in education should occur 'with all deliberate speed' — failed to specify exactly when it should happen.

Why did early NAACP campaigns focus on education?

The Brown case and Brown II (1954–55) were two high-profile examples of the NAACP in action. The NAACP focused on education because this was an area in which it could be clearly demonstrated that black and white citizens were not being treated as equals. For example, it was possible to compare class sizes, resource levels, teachers' salaries and state funding. Classes in white schools, for instance, were smaller by a third than those in black schools. Additionally, in South Carolina in 1949 an average of $179 was spent on the education of each white child but only $43 was spent on each black student.

The NAACP also focused on education because it was believed that changing the educational opportunities of black students was the first step towards improving their employment opportunities and thus their social and economic status. Moreover, educated black citizens would be better equipped to fight for their civil rights. Finally, the treatment of children was an emotive issue. Consequently, the NAACP was likely to have public backing when challenging inequalities in education.

Achievements of early NAACP campaigns

In spite of the NAACP's legal success in the early 1950s, substantial change was slow to follow. By 1956, 250,000 white people had joined citizens' councils to protest against the desegregation of schools. Additionally, by 1957, only 750 of over 6,000 schools districts in the south had been desegregated. Consequently, by 1957, 97% of black students remained in segregated schools.

The NAACP had also started legal campaigns concerning voting rights and transport. The political rights of black Americans were an essential part of the civil rights agenda, and in the case of *Smith* v *Allwright* (1944), the NAACP successfully established that the all-white **primary elections** held by the Democratic Party in Texas broke the provisions of the **15th Amendment**. The NAACP argued that as the Democratic Party's hold on Texas was so strong, the primary election effectively selected the winning candidate. In transport, the NAACP's victory in the case of *Morgan* v *Virginia* (1946) established that segregation was illegal on interstate transport. However, the legal victory was opposed by businesses, local politicians and the public, and therefore full segregation of interstate transport did not occur until the 1960s.

Signs of change by 1955

By 1955, the NAACP had grown substantially and won a series of important legal victories. Additionally, President Truman had given support to civil rights initiatives and brought about changes in government policy in an attempt to win the support of black voters. The establishment of CORE in 1942 was also significant because it showed the increasing radicalisation of black citizens and because it pioneered an alternative strategy to the legal campaigns of the NAACP.

However, the success of CORE and the NAACP was limited. The NAACP's legal victories did not translate easily into *de facto* change. This demonstrated that success in the courts did not necessarily produce a change in the deeply entrenched racist attitudes that characterised much of US society.

Glossary

14th Amendment: an addition to the US constitution in 1868 stating that anybody born in the USA has the full rights of citizenship and that no state government can take these rights away.

15th Amendment: an addition to the US constitution in 1870 stating that all citizens have the right to vote, regardless of their colour.

Cold War: an ideological conflict between capitalist USA and the communist USSR following the end of the Second World War. The Cold War was also characterised by international tension between capitalist and communist countries, which occasionally turned into military conflict, for example in the Vietnam War.

de facto: *de facto* segregation occurs when African Americans and whites are segregated in non-legal ways, such as living in separate housing areas and attending different schools. *De facto* segregation occurred across the USA outside the Old South and areas where Jim Crow laws had been passed.

de jure: *de jure* segregation is segregation backed by law, either state or federal.

emancipation: the act of liberation.

grandfather clauses: following the 15th Amendment, southern states introduced laws to exclude black people from voting which were not based on race. The grandfather clause excluded people whose grandfathers had not been enfranchised.

Ku Klux Klan: a white supremacist organisation, founded in the nineteenth century and dedicated to overturning the rights won by black people following the American Civil War. The group was most influential in the southern states.

literacy tests: following the 15th Amendment, southern states introduced laws to exclude black people from voting which were not based on race. Literacy tests excluded all those who were unable to read and write. However, in practice, illiterate whites were permitted to vote and the law was applied only to black citizens.

primary elections: elections held by the Democrat and Republican parties in which voters select the candidates from each party to be entered for subsequent elections.

sharecroppers: small-scale farmers who are leased land by landowners in return for a percentage of their crop.

sit-ins: a form of non-violent protest in which activists refuse to leave an area until their demands are met.

Supreme Court: the highest court of appeal in the USA. The court has the right to strike down any laws that it believes to be unconstitutional.

1955–68: Martin Luther King and peaceful protest

Martin Luther King's background and ideology

Martin Luther King was born in Atlanta, Georgia in 1929, and enjoyed a relatively privileged upbringing. He graduated from Morehouse College with a degree in sociology in 1948, and then attended Crozier Theological Seminary, and finally the University of Boston, where in 1955 he received his PhD in theology. Prior to his involvement in the civil rights movement, he was, like his father, a Baptist minister.

King's education and religious beliefs informed his approach to the civil rights struggle and his aspirations for his fellow black citizens. Christianity inspired King's aims and his methods. He believed that the campaign for civil rights was God's will, as God had created all humanity in his own image. Moreover, Jesus's message of compassion and non-retaliation characterised King's non-violent approach to protest and his political opponents. Additionally, King believed that civil rights could, and should, be realised by working within the constitution. Indeed, his goal was to ensure that the rhetoric of the **Bill of Rights** and the Declaration of Independence applied equally to all citizens. Consequently, King was willing to work closely with the federal government as well as Presidents Kennedy and Johnson.

King's vision was a society in which black citizens were able to take a full part in and enjoy all the benefits of US culture. In this sense King wanted to integrate black people fully into US society. King's dream stands in stark contrast to Malcolm X's agenda, which claimed that US society was so corrupt that integration would be harmful to African Americans.

Peaceful protest

Martin Luther King adopted the method of peaceful protest for three main reasons. First, he believed peaceful protest was a fundamentally Christian approach to political activity. Secondly, he hoped that by organising events such as boycotts and sit-ins, he would attract media attention, and thereby expose racist policies and laws to the public. Finally, he hoped that his peaceful campaigns would gain public sympathy, because the dignity of the protesters would stand in stark contrast to the racism of those who opposed them.

Additionally, peaceful protest was adopted to enforce the rulings on desegregation that had come about as a result of the work of the NAACP. In this way, the NAACP's achievement from 1945 to 1960 is paradoxical. The main thrust of its campaign was to legally overturn the Jim Crow laws. While it succeeded in doing this, this achievement on its own did not end *de facto* segregation in America's south. Rather, the NAACP was more successful in inspiring young activists who chose quite a different strategy, allying themselves with the non-violent, civil disobedience campaigns of the Southern Christian Leadership Conference (SCLC), the Student Non-violent Coordinating Committee (SNCC) and the Congress of Racial Equality (CORE).

The focus of the campaigns

Transport

Jim Crow laws segregated public transport in the southern states. In 1955–56 there were two parallel attempts to desegregate public transport. First, there was a public campaign of peaceful protest, which began when Rosa Parks (a long-standing member of the NAACP) was legally obliged to move when a white passenger wanted a seat on a bus. Her refusal to move led to her arrest and prosecution, and sparked the Montgomery bus boycott. The boycott was an attempt by black Americans to force the desegregation of public transport, and lasted for over a year. Secondly, the NAACP mounted a legal challenge (*Browder* v *Gayle*) to the Montgomery and Alabama transport segregation laws.

The boycott was significant for a number of reasons. First, it provided a platform for the emerging leader of the US civil rights movement, Dr Martin Luther King. Secondly, it led to the creation of another important civil rights organisation, the Southern Christian Leadership Conference, in 1957. Thirdly, the scale of the protest was effective in gaining widespread media attention. Nonetheless, it was the legal challenge, and not the boycott, that ended segregation on the buses in 1956.

The NAACP also sought the nationwide desegregation of buses and bus terminals. The Supreme Court case *Morgan* v *Virginia* (1946) had ruled that segregation on interstate travel was unconstitutional. A second case, *Boynton* v *Virginia* (1960), established that segregation in public transport terminal facilities was also illegal.

CORE and the newly formed Student Non-violent Coordinating Committee put this ruling to the test almost immediately, organising the Freedom Rides of 1961. CORE's mixed-race team attempted to travel from Washington DC to New Orleans on inter-state buses. In both Anniston and Birmingham, Alabama, the SNCC team were victims of racist attacks. Notably, the local police were indifferent to these assaults. The Freedom Rides were significant as they provided a context for cooperation between the chief civil rights organisations, CORE, the SNCC and the SCLC. Additionally, they focused media attention on the continuing activity of racist groups such as the KKK.

Finally, President Kennedy (1961–63) was forced to address the issues. Federal injunctions were brought out against the KKK, and Attorney-General Robert Kennedy ordered the desegregation of all inter-state travel. On the other hand, federal government's sympathy for the civil rights movement was qualified. Indeed, federal government continued to support the imprisonment of civil rights protesters as long as white attackers were dealt with in the same way.

Education

In 1957, nine African-American students set out to test the legal ruling on educational integration that had been brought about by the Brown case. In order to do this, they enrolled at Little Rock Central High School, Arkansas. A crisis erupted when Governor Orville Faubus ordered the **National Guard** to surround the school and keep the 'Little Rock Nine' out. President Eisenhower (1953–61) responded by sending in federal troops to enforce desegregation. Nonetheless, Governor Faubus was not prepared to admit defeat, and consequently closed the school rather than accept integration.

Challenges to segregation in education were extended to universities in the early 1960s. In 1961, violent protests greeted James Meredith's attempts to enrol at the University of Mississippi. Robert Kennedy, US Attorney-General, supported Meredith's enrolment. At the same time, the state governor, Ross Barnett, publicly protested against the move. Following Meredith's admission to the university, the campus was desegregated. However, in spite of the legal ruling of Brown and the peaceful protests at Little Rock and the University of Mississippi, by 1968 only 42% of US black students were attending desegregated schools.

Social and economic change

Segregation was a fact of life that extended beyond education and transport. In the south, restaurants, libraries, parks and other local amenities were routinely segregated. By 1960 this segregation was no longer lawful, but it continued due to the obstinacy of southern whites. Moreover, discrimination was widely practised in employment. The early 1960s saw a series of peaceful campaigns aimed largely at challenging this social and economic segregation.

In 1960, the SNCC organised sit-ins in Greensboro, North Carolina, to protest against the unlawful segregation of a local Woolworth's canteen. Protesters were refused service but no attempt was made to evict them. This sit-in sparked a series of similar sit-ins, swim-ins, read-ins and economic boycotts which in 2 months spread to 54 cities in nine states, with 50,000 people actively involved. By the end of 1961, over 800 towns and cities had desegregated public areas.

A further step was taken in 1961 when President Kennedy issued Executive Order 10925. This established the President's Committee on Equal Employment Opportunity and legally ended discrimination in all appointments by the federal government and its contractors and subcontractors. The order also gave the government the power to prosecute offenders and issue a 'certificate of merit' to any organisation that was shown to be an equal opportunities employer.

Following Greensboro, non-violent methods were applied to Albany, Georgia (1961–62), and Birmingham, Alabama (1963), in an attempt to overturn racial discrimination. In both cases, non-violent protests were designed to provoke racist violence, and thereby focus media attention on the ongoing struggle for equality.

In Birmingham, this strategy proved highly successful. Local police chief Eugene 'Bull' Connor used water cannon, dogs and heavy-handed policing against unarmed protesters. To avoid the economic disruption of more boycotts, Birmingham stores began to desegregate and businesses pledged to end discriminatory employment practices. In addition, media portrayal of the protests and Connor's response attracted increased support from those outside the south.

By contrast, the Albany campaign, a year earlier, had not been a success. Police chief Laurie Pritchett ensured that the police treated the protesters with respect. He also agreed to discussions about the end of segregation in the city. This effectively defused the situation without leading to any concrete gains for Albany's black citizens.

The March on Washington in August 1963 was staged to draw attention to issues of segregation and black economic conditions. A quarter of a million protesters descended on Washington DC to hear Martin Luther King's famous 'I Have a Dream' speech. The march was significant as it marked a moment of unity between the different strands of the civil rights movement and the Kennedy administration. Moreover, the March on Washington was one of the factors that led to the passing of the Civil Rights Act of 1964 under the Presidency of Lyndon B. Johnson (1963–69). Essentially, the Act banned segregation and gave the government powers to enforce this ban. In addition, it created a Fair Employment Practices Commission to address discrimination in the workplace. Economic discrimination was also explicitly outlawed in any projects supported by the federal government.

The Civil Rights Act (1964) and the Voting Rights Act (1965) did not mark the end of King's vision, but they did lead to a change in direction for the movement. As the 1965 government-commissioned Moynihan Report revealed, black Americans throughout the USA still faced considerable social and economic hardships. For this reason, King turned his attention to issues of poverty, and moved his focus to the northern states where problems of **ghettoisation** were especially severe. In addition, King and the SCLC hoped to encourage the use of peaceful protest outside the southern states.

Poor housing conditions, increased racial disturbances and a lack of racial integration led King to choose the northern city of Chicago, Illinois, as the focus for his 1966 campaign. King's strategy for dealing with ghettoisation in the north was essentially the same as his strategy for dealing with formal segregation in the south. However, as in Albany, Mayor Richard Daley refused to play into his hands, instead making ambiguous promises about improving housing conditions, and implicitly rejecting King's involvement. Additionally, King was unfamiliar with northern conditions and did not enjoy the same respect from, and rapport with, northern African Americans.

In spite of the setback in Chicago, King's final campaign was more ambitious still. The Poor People's Campaign was intended, in King's words, to unite poor people of all races in an attempt to 'confront the power structure'. King believed that a broader coalition was necessary to confront poverty because economic advancement for black

Americans could take place only at the expense of the rich, and therefore the most powerful, people in the USA. In this sense, the battle against poverty would be much more difficult than the battle against segregation, and therefore needed a greater degree of popular support.

Political rights

The year 1965 saw King and the SCLC challenge the political exclusion of black Americans in Selma, Alabama, where only 335 of over 15,000 African Americans were registered to vote. This was an important test of the influence of the Civil Rights Act in the south. The Selma authorities, headed by Sheriff Jim Clark, obstructed the registration of black voters with a series of qualifying questions such as 'How many bubbles are there in a bar of soap?' Additionally, the Selma police used electric cattle prods to try and disperse black citizens who were queuing to vote. This ill treatment, coupled with a series of marches from Selma to Montgomery, drew media attention to the continuing disenfranchisement of southern African Americans. President Johnson responded with the Voting Rights Act (1965).

Evaluating the success of peaceful protest

Direct action helped to change the law and was used to test the implementation of these laws. During the Montgomery bus boycott (1956), the Greensboro sit-ins (1960) and the Birmingham campaign (1963), direct action proved particularly successful at winning public support for racial integration. Peaceful protest gave activists the moral high ground. This was especially evident in Birmingham, where media coverage contrasted the brutality of the white police with the dignity of the black protesters. The change in public opinion helped convince law-makers, locally and federally, that reform was necessary. Peaceful protest, then, achieved the destruction of Jim Crow laws in a number of major cities in the south.

Aside from changing the law, peaceful protest sought to test it. During the Freedom Rides (1961), for example, non-violent direct action sought to realise the legal gains of the NAACP campaigns, thus seeking to bring *de facto* change out of *de jure* victory. Similarly, Little Rock (1957) tested the Brown ruling of 2 years before. In this way, direct action was used to accelerate the disintegration of segregation by forcibly bringing practice into line with Supreme Court rulings.

The cumulative effect of peaceful protest in the early 1960s helped to create the public support and political will to enact the Civil Rights Act (1964) and the Voting Rights Act (1965). These Acts had national significance and underlined the effectiveness of non-violent campaigning.

On the other hand, peaceful protest was not always successful. It increasingly came to rely on provoking a violent response from over-zealous white authorities. In cases where the local authorities were shrewd and refused to be provoked, little change was evident. Albany (1961–62), for example, failed to effect any meaningful change for precisely this reason.

Secondly, non-violent direct action essentially failed to bring about social and economic change. King's Chicago campaign (1966) achieved nothing more than vague promises from Chicago's mayor, Richard Daley. King acknowledged that effecting social and economic change was necessarily harder than challenging segregation, as the former was both costly and not simply a matter of changing the law.

Finally, it is also notable that even after the Selma campaign and the Voting Rights Act of 1965, the proportion of black citizens registered to vote never equalled the proportion of registered white voters. By the end of 1966, four out of the 13 southern states still had fewer than 50% of African Americans registered to vote.

Opposition to equal rights

Opposition to the civil rights movement came from a variety of powerful sources, such as US presidents, Congress, local state authorities, and the police and Federal Bureau of Investigation (FBI). Additionally, white citizens, taking their lead from these authorities, tried to obstruct the progress of racial integration.

Presidential opposition

Neither of the US presidents in the period 1955–63 gave civil rights their full support. Eisenhower, for example, was particularly reluctant to support the campaign for racial equality. He was unwilling to show clear leadership on issues relating to civil rights, as he was aware that it could lose him the support of white voters. Moreover, he was born and raised in the segregated south and shared the assumptions of many of the white racists. He regarded the activities of groups such as the SCLC as unduly aggressive and therefore sympathised with white southerners who felt threatened by civil rights campaigns.

Eisenhower's presidency spanned a number of major events in the civil rights campaign, such as the Brown case, the Montgomery bus boycott, the Little Rock campaign, the Greensboro sit-ins and the Freedom Rides. However, he had little sympathy with these campaigns and only met with King and other black leaders once. He refused to give federal support to the Montgomery bus boycott and, until the events of Little Rock, declined to use federal power to enforce the Brown decision.

Moreover, Eisenhower and Kennedy were both dependent on the support of southern senators who opposed desegregation. In order to appease these senators, both presidents were cautious, although Kennedy was prepared to make radical moves when he felt he had sufficient public support.

Opposition in Congress

Congressional opposition to civil rights measures began in earnest in 1956, when 101 southern congressmen signed the 'Southern Manifesto'. The manifesto strongly criticised the Supreme Court's decisions in the Brown case, arguing that they represented a 'clear abuse of judicial power'.

Eisenhower's attempt to pass a Civil Rights Act in 1960 was also severely hampered by congressmen from both parties. Southern senators opposed the bill as it would lead to major changes in their segregated constituencies. One congressional strategy to defeat the bill was to table a series of amendments that would weaken it. Even the weakened Act was more than some southern senators were prepared to endorse. As a result, South Carolina's Senator J. Strom Thurmond spoke for 24 hours and 18 minutes against the bill. This technique of talking until the bill runs out of congressional time, known as a filibuster, failed. Nonetheless, the bill had been so weakened that it achieved little for African Americans.

Kennedy and Johnson had more support from Congress for their civil rights initiatives. In spite of this, however, they faced strong opposition from southern senators. For example, all 10 southern Republican members of the House of Representatives and 87 of 94 southern Democrat members voted against the 1964 Civil Rights Act.

Opposition from state authorities and the local police

The US constitution distinguishes between 'state' and 'federal' government. Federal government, headed by the president and based in Washington DC, is responsible for matters that affect the whole of the USA. However, state governments have considerable independence concerning local laws. Indeed, it was the independence of local governments in the southern states that allowed Jim Crow laws to emerge in the nineteenth century.

Civil rights campaigners met opposition from state governors and local authorities in southern and northern states. This opposition took one of two forms. First, in campaigns such as Little Rock and Birmingham, state governors and other local officials used their power to block desegregation in a highly public and confrontational manner. In Birmingham, for example, police chief 'Bull' Connor used water cannon, plastic bullets and other forms of violent physical intimidation in an attempt to break up peaceful protest. However, these tactics were counterproductive, as they guaranteed media interest and, in so doing, won public sympathy for the protesters.

A second strategy, which was more effective at countering the protests, was adopted in Albany and Chicago. In these cases, state governors and local authorities treated protesters with apparent respect, and diffused difficult situations by making vague promises of change. This strategy gave the media less of an incentive to cover the protests and did not provoke public interest.

Opposition from the Federal Bureau of Investigation

The federal police, or FBI, were also opponents of the civil rights movement. The FBI was concerned about the activities of Stanley Levison and Jack O'Dell, who worked closely with Martin Luther King and the SCLC. Levison and O'Dell had both been members of the Communist Party and J. Edgar Hoover, head of the FBI, believed that the SCLC was a front for Communist Party activity. In the climate of the Cold War, Hoover believed that US communists, working with the Soviet government, were planning a communist takeover of the US government.

Robert Kennedy, the attorney-general from 1960 to 1963, gave the FBI the authority to investigate the SCLC. Consequently, the FBI bugged telephone calls and burgled the offices of lawyers who worked for Levison and O'Dell. Through these activities, the FBI was able to establish that O'Dell had been a communist, and caused King and the SCLC significant damage by leaking this information to the *New York Times*.

White opposition

The civil rights campaigners faced racism from white Americans throughout their campaigns. An example of this is the White Citizens' Councils formed in the deep south in response to the Brown case. Further evidence of racism can be found in the Little Rock incident, where violent confrontations between hysterical white mobs and black students had to be controlled by the National Guard. Worse still was the treatment of NAACP official Medgar Evers, who was assassinated by a white extremist at his home in Mississippi during the Birmingham campaign.

Violent white racism was not limited to the southern states. King's Chicago campaign also met white resistance, with protesters being attacked with broken bottles and bricks. Indeed, King observed that the bitterness of white reaction in Chicago was even more extreme than it had been in the south.

Martin Luther King: saint or sinner?

King was and is a controversial figure. Questions about his effectiveness as a leader, his relationship with the white authorities, his ability to understand the difficulties faced by working-class African Americans and his moral character dog his legacy.

King rose to national prominence during the Montgomery bus boycott of 1955–56. However, the bus boycott was initiated by local NAACP activists. Some in the NAACP claimed that King effectively hijacked the campaign to further his own reputation. King faced similar criticisms from the leaders of the Greensboro sit-ins in 1960. In addition, King's poor organisational skills jeopardised the effectiveness of the SCLC's campaigns. It has been argued that while King was highly effective at grabbing headlines and acting as a figurehead for the movement, he was poorly equipped to coordinate sustained local campaigns. King's inspirational idealism was not allied with practical administrative skills. For example, the 1957 Crusade for Citizenship (an attempt to persuade federal government to guarantee voting rights for African Americans) suffered as it was not supported by a sufficient number of salaried staff. In addition, the Chicago campaign was accused of having no clear objectives and raising expectations that could not be met.

King was not universally respected by African-American leaders. His refusal to sanction violent methods, the fact that he advocated 'turning the other cheek' and his sometimes close relationship with Presidents Kennedy and Johnson led some African Americans to liken King to the fictional character **Uncle Tom**. By this they meant that King adopted a slavish attitude to the white authorities, and that this was detrimental to the struggle of black Americans.

The accusation that King was an 'Uncle Tom' was heightened by his perceived failure to understand the difficulties faced by working-class African Americans. King's own background was relatively privileged. He had never experienced many of the social and economic difficulties against which he campaigned. This was particularly pronounced during his northern campaigns. Furthermore, King's Christian philosophy was not shared by the majority of African Americans in the north. This further underlined the differences between King and the people he sought to represent.

Finally, King was criticised for failing to live up to his Christian standards in his personal life. King had a series of affairs which were seen by some as undermining his moral position.

However, while it is clear that King was not perfect, he was undoubtedly an extraordinary individual. King possessed an ability to inspire black and white audiences through stirring oratory. He may not have personally experienced some of the oppression he fought, but he had the ability to articulate the feelings of many African Americans. King's famous 'I have a dream' speech (1963) is a clear example of King's outstanding ability as a speaker.

King's ability to inspire went beyond his powerful speeches. King's courage in the face of police brutality, racist violence and jail encouraged many activists to continue fighting. For example, King stood firm when confronted by 30–40 threatening letters a day and the fire-bombing of his own home during the Montgomery bus boycott.

King's ability to manipulate the media was perhaps his greatest strength. King did not invent peaceful protest, but he did realise that it was significantly more powerful in the age of mass media. The images of peaceful resistance to racist violence shocked the USA and swung public opinion behind King's campaigns. This technique was employed to great effect in Birmingham in 1963. King's achievement was recognised in 1964 when he was awarded the Nobel Peace Prize.

King's leadership was not without its critics. Nevertheless, King's oratory, courage and ability to inspire made him the ideal figurehead for the civil rights movement.

Legal changes and the role of federal government

Civil rights campaigners often looked to federal government to advance their cause. Jim Crow laws were peculiar to the southern states and could therefore be over-ruled by federal bodies. During the period 1955–68 there were three US presidents: Eisenhower, Kennedy and Johnson.

Dwight D. Eisenhower (1953–61)

Broadly speaking, Eisenhower took the view that race relations would improve of their own accord over time. This is illustrated by his reluctance to intervene in the events at Little Rock in 1957. The exceptions to this hands-off approach were Eisenhower's Civil Rights Acts of 1957 and 1960. Eisenhower proposed legislation to guarantee the vote to all citizens and to establish a special division of the Justice Department to deal with civil rights. However, when the bill was attacked by southern Democratic senators, Eisenhower backed down. Consequently, the 1957 Civil Rights Act was significantly watered down: for example, the Act specified that white officials who denied black citizens the right to vote could be tried by all-white juries.

Eisenhower tried again in the late 1950s, but between them, his two Civil Rights Bills had added a mere 3% of black voters to the electoral rolls by the end of 1960. Eisenhower's motivation for the Civil Rights Bills was the impending presidential elections. Here his goal was to win the black vote without alienating the southern white vote. This motivation goes some way to explain why the bills promised much and delivered little.

John F. Kennedy (1961–63)

During his presidential campaign, Kennedy claimed that racism was a moral evil and pledged to help African-American citizens. Kennedy's phone call to Coretta King, while her husband was in prison during the Birmingham campaign, did much to persuade black voters that Kennedy was sympathetic to their cause. However, once in office he took no immediate action, concentrating instead on legislation to improve healthcare and poverty. Kennedy was concerned that focusing on civil rights would alienate southern congressmen and jeopardise his healthcare and poverty legislation.

Kennedy's action on civil right was mainly symbolic. For example, he appointed five black federal judges including the NAACP's chief counsel Thurgood Marshall, and he invited more African Americans to the White House than any previous president. Additionally, he created the Committee on Equal Employment Opportunity (CEEO), which was mandated to ensure equal employment opportunities for the employees of federal government. However, the success of the CEEO was easily exaggerated. An increase of two black employees in a government office could, for example, be presented as a 100% increase in the employment of African Americans.

Kennedy's sympathies for civil rights broadly followed public opinion. In the late 1950s, he opposed Eisenhower's Civil Rights Bills for political reasons. However, as the public became increasingly interested in civil rights issues, his attitude softened. Essentially, Kennedy was reluctant to show leadership on civil rights issues. Nonetheless, the success of civil rights campaigns could force Kennedy to take action. For example, Kennedy refused to press for an end to segregation in Birmingham until King's campaign had provoked public outrage at the treatment of African Americans in the city.

Kennedy's approach to civil rights legislation is typical of his general approach. He committed himself to a civil rights bill during his election campaign. However, he took no action until June 1963. Even then, the March on Washington was necessary to persuade Kennedy to make the bill a priority. By the end of 1963, however, Kennedy was prepared to risk his political career and support the bill.

Lyndon B. Johnson (1963–69)

Johnson became president following Kennedy's assassination in November 1963. During the 1950s, Johnson was a firm supporter of the Supreme Court's rulings on the Brown case, and he later orchestrated the passing of Eisenhower's Civil Rights Acts. Johnson was fully committed to passing the Civil Rights Act of 1964: he went as far as to say that he would sacrifice his chances of re-election, if necessary, to pass the Act. Although the Act's success has been attributed to Kennedy's campaign and public sympathy following Kennedy's death, it was Johnson's tireless agitation in the Senate that ensured the bill's success.

Following the Selma campaign, Johnson also proposed and ensured the passage of the Voting Rights Act (1965). This Act outlawed any tests that excluded US citizens from voting, such as literacy tests, or tests that assessed the educational qualifications or moral character of potential voters. In the mid-1960s Johnson publicly collaborated with King on both of these bills.

Johnson's commitment to civil rights is also evident in his educational reforms. The Elementary and Secondary Education Act (1965) and the Higher Education Act (1965) increased the funding given to education provision in poorer states, leading to the quadrupling of black college students between 1965 and 1975. Finally, Johnson's 1968 Civil Rights Act sought to outlaw racial discrimination in the housing market. The Act prohibited discrimination in housing provision on the basis of race, nationality, religion and gender.

Johnson was ideologically committed to a vision of the USA as 'The Great Society'. An end to racism was at the heart of this vision. He claimed that 'The Great Society rests on abundance and liberty for all. It demands an end to poverty and racial injustice, to which we are totally committed in our time.' He was aware that legislation alone could not secure equality and that 'affirmative action' was needed before African Americans could be truly equal.

Johnson undoubtedly achieved more than any of his predecessors in advancing the cause of racial equality. However, as US involvement in the Vietnam War increased, Johnson's attention, and the government's budget, moved away from civil rights towards the war in Vietnam.

Congress and the Supreme Court

Congress, the USA's supreme law-making body, had a significant role to play in advancing African-American rights between 1945 and 1968. Initially, Congress resisted legal changes in favour of African Americans. However, by the mid-1960s Congress was prepared to pass a series of important Acts. For example, 73 of the 100 senators, and 289 of the 435 members of the House of Representatives voted in favour of the Civil Rights Act of 1964. Similarly, the 1968 Civil Rights Act passed with 71 votes in the Senate and 250 votes in the House of Representatives.

The Supreme Court was also a significant factor in overturning segregation. In 1953, President Eisenhower appointed Earl Warren as Chief Justice of the Supreme Court. Warren's sympathy for the plight of African Americans was evident in cases such as Brown, Brown II and *Browder* v *Gayle*. Between 1954 and 1960, under Warren's leadership, the Supreme Court made a series of landmark judgements which paved the way for the Civil Rights Act of 1964, and the consequent end of segregation in the south. Warren's impact was such that Eisenhower later remarked that his appointment 'was the biggest damned fool mistake I've ever made in my life'.

Glossary

Bill of Rights: the first ten amendments to the US constitution, guaranteeing the rights of freedom of speech, freedom of assembly and freedom of conscience.

ghettoisation: the isolation of black people in a specific geographical area, often with relatively poor facilities.

National Guard: a military force designed for home defence. It is a national organisation, but it is organised along state lines, so that in normal circumstances it is available for the state governor to call upon in times of emergency. However, it remains under the ultimate control of the president, acting as commander-in-chief of all the armed forces.

Uncle Tom: a fictional black character appearing in the book *Uncle Tom's Cabin* by Harriet Beecher Stowe (1852) who was characterised by his devotion to his white owners. The term became an insult and was applied to Martin Luther King following his collaboration with Kennedy and Johnson.

1960–68: Black Power and the use of violence

Unity and divisions in the civil rights movement, 1960–66

Working together

There had always been differences between the various groups campaigning for black civil rights. In the late 1950s and early 1960s the groups worked together successfully in a number of campaigns. However, there were tensions in the relationships between groups with different aims, methods and ideologies.

The non-violent arm of the civil rights movement was made up of a variety of different groups. These included the NAACP, CORE, the SCLC and the SNCC. The NAACP and CORE were the oldest political groups fighting segregation. Their aims were broadly similar, but their methods were quite different. The NAACP chose to advance civil rights through legal actions, challenging existing legislation. CORE, by contrast, was the first civil rights organisation to explore direct action, such as the sit-ins of the early 1960s. In this sense, it was far more confrontational than the older, more conservative, NAACP.

In addition to CORE, other groups embracing direct action were the SCLC and SNCC. The SCLC shared the NAACP's desire to work within the US system, and it sought to work with the NAACP on public transport and voter registration issues. However, the SCLC deliberately refused to accept individual members, as this was part of the NAACP's strategy and the SCLC did not want to be seen as a rival organisation.

The SNCC was formed in 1960 following the Greensboro sit-ins. It was different from the other groups, as it focused on encouraging student participation in civil rights campaigns. From the start it was more militant than the older organisations. The SNCC's strategy was deliberately to provoke crisis situations that would force action on the part of state and federal government.

The year 1963 saw the establishment of the Coordinating Council of Community Organisations (CCCO). This brought the NAACP, CORE, the SCLC and the SNCC together in a joint campaign to further educational integration. The CCCO represents the high point of cooperation between the four groups.

Increasing divisions

In the months following the foundation of the CCCO, relations between the four groups began to deteriorate. By 1963 the NAACP's legal campaign appeared to have run its course and the focus shifted to the demands for *de facto* change. Consequently, direct action was seen as a more appropriate method and the NAACP's influence declined.

After 1964 CORE turned to more militant campaigns for employment rights in the north. CORE's change of tactics stemmed from its realisation that its peaceful campaigns had only helped middle-class black people, and militancy was seen as a way of helping the black working class. This, sometimes violent, militancy marked a divergence from the SCLC, which remained committed to exclusively peaceful methods. The SNCC also deliberately distanced itself from the SCLC to counter the perception that it was essentially the student wing of King's organisation. Between 1961 and 1964, the SNCC focused on non-violent direct action to achieve integration. This included sit-ins and in 1964 voter registration campaigns.

Explaining the rise of black militancy

By the mid-1960s, the black movement was clearly split between those still committed to non-violence, and more radical groups which believed that more militant methods were necessary to fight white oppression.

King's failures

First, black militancy was increasingly attractive because of King's apparent failures in the late 1960s. Disillusionment with King's methods was evident in the Watts Riots in Los Angeles in 1965. The black community of Los Angeles had the legal right to use the same amenities and live in the same areas as white citizens. However, due to widespread black poverty, these rights remained largely theoretical. Many felt that King's victories in the south had done little to improve living conditions elsewhere. Resentment at these conditions turned into violence following the arrest and brutal treatment of Marquette Frye for alleged drink-driving. Over 6 days, $40 million worth of destruction occurred, 14,000 troops were required to restore order, 4,000 people were arrested, and 34 people were killed.

Furthermore, in the late 1960s, King's non-violent methods seemed to be increasingly ineffective. The Chicago campaign, for example, achieved little more than a paper victory. Moreover, the SCLC was given a government grant of $4 million to help improve ghetto housing. This led local African Americans to claim that King and the SCLC had been bought off by the government, further discrediting King. African Americans in the north felt forced to look elsewhere for a movement that would truly represent them.

Black separatism

The position of white supporters of black civil rights changed in the mid-1960s. Many white liberals who had supported the southern campaigns believed that the victories of 1964 and 1965 were sufficient to guarantee black freedom and equality, and therefore saw no need for further campaigns. What is more, black radicals began to question the effectiveness of working with white sympathisers. The year 1964 was a turning point for the SNCC, as its efforts to establish the Mississippi Freedom Democratic Party were vetoed by the Democratic National Convention. Following this, the SNCC refused to work in coalition with whites and advocated black separatism rather than racial integration. In 1966, the SNCC published a position paper in the *New York Times* which stated that white people had no further role in the black movement.

SNCC embraces Black Power

Divisions within the civil rights movement also contributed to black militancy. For example, the 'March Against Fear' in 1966 witnessed an assassination attempt on James Meredith. Meredith's original intention had been to use the march to encourage black voter registration across the southern states. However, following his shooting, leading members of the SNCC continued with a more radical agenda. SNCC members on the march began the chant 'Black Power! Black Power!' and adopted the logo of the clenched fist. Stokely Carmichael also encouraged violence towards property when he advocated the burning of every courthouse in Mississippi.

The march marked a turning point in the relationship between the SNCC on the one hand, and the SCLC and the NAACP on the other. The SNCC refused to work with the SCLC because it believed the latter was run by a middle-class black elite who tended to impose their organisation and strategies on the communities in which they worked. The SNCC, on the other hand, emphasised the importance of local grass-roots activism. Its strategy was to encourage black people to organise themselves.

These divisions led to polarisation within the movement. King was no longer able to exert any influence over the radicals in the SNCC, and their militancy could continue unchecked.

A new leader

By the early 1960s, almost 70% of the USA's black population lived in central city ghettos. Working-class African Americans found it difficult to identify with Martin Luther King because of his middle-class education and southern roots. They felt that King did not understand the problems that they were facing, and they also had little sympathy with his Christian message.

Malcolm X, leading spokesman for the radical black organisation, the **Nation of Islam**, was a much more appealing figure for many urban black Americans, mainly in the north. They felt that Malcolm X understood their problems and aspirations due to the fact that his working-class background was similar to their own: he had spent his childhood in an urban ghetto. In this way, Malcolm X's background increased support for his militant message and tactics.

Cultural radicalisation

Black militancy was also part of a general cultural liberalisation among students and young people. This was evident in new attitudes to sexual relationships, hallucinogenic drugs and psychedelic music culture. Young people became more interested in experimental and even revolutionary lifestyles. From this perspective, the traditional civil rights movements such as the NAACP and the SCLC were too conservative, committed as they were to working with the establishment.

The impact of the Vietnam War

The Vietnam War had a considerable impact on the progress of the civil rights movement and the emergence of Black Power groups. First, the war had an undoubted economic impact on US society. The cost of supplying almost 400,000 US troops diverted resources away from Johnson's social and economic policies, which had been designed to address inner-city poverty.

Secondly, the Vietnam War divided communities and hardened attitudes. Indeed, when King spoke out against the Vietnam War in 1967, many white Americans felt that he had acted unpatriotically and therefore King lost the support of some sections in the white community. The war also soured the relationship between King and Johnson. Johnson was committed to the war because of his desire to stop the spread of communism. King, on the other hand, was deeply suspicious of all violent action because of his commitment to Christianity.

Thirdly, the ongoing conflict and protests against the war dominated the media and therefore removed attention from later civil rights campaigns.

Finally, many black Americans were struck by the contradiction of fighting for democracy abroad while they continued to experience racism and discrimination at home. What is more, black leaders criticised the federal government for sending thousands of soldiers to fight in Asia, while black Americans were unprotected from racial attacks in the USA.

Black Power

The Black Power movement

The Black Power movement (a term that is used to describe the Black Panthers and the followers of Malcolm X, as well as CORE and the SNCC after 1964) believed that the non-violent civil rights movement of the 1950s and early 1960s had failed to address the real issues affecting black people. Moreover, they believed that the strategy of working with white people for formal legal changes would never achieve black emancipation. Malcolm X's call to fight white oppression 'by all means necessary' characterised their militant methodology. Nonetheless, it would be incorrect to view Black Power as a coherent movement with shared aims and ideals. Rather, the phrase is used as a blanket term to describe disparate groups who shared the belief that the black community should reject the goal of racial integration and the methods of non-violence, in favour of black nationalism.

Self-determination

Malcolm X, and the Nation of Islam, advocated the principles of **self-determination** and Black Pride. Malcolm X linked self-determination to black freedom by arguing that black people could only be free in an all-black community. In this sense, King's dream of racial integration was Malcolm X's nightmare. Integration would simply lead to the corruption of black people by whites. Indeed, he accused white liberals of being hypocrites. However, Malcolm X was unclear whether this all-black community would be a separate nation within North America, or whether a return to Africa was necessary.

Black Pride, for Malcolm X, meant that black people would only gain freedom by their own efforts and hard work. Malcolm X broke with the Nation of Islam in 1964, leading to his assassination by members of the Nation of Islam in 1965.

The SNCC advocated a similar agenda, which it described as 'Black Power'. This was a slogan coined by Stokely Carmichael, a prominent member of the SNCC. The expulsion of white members from the SNCC was the first step towards self-determination. However, full self-determination would only be achieved when African Americans became the 'New Afrikans'. By this Carmichael meant that black Americans should establish an independent nation within the territory of the USA, in which they would form the majority. He argued that this was the only way in which black people could take control of their own lives.

Self-determination was appealing to many black radicals because the clear rejection of any alliance with white citizens or the 'white government' meant that figures like Malcolm X could never be described as 'a tool of the white man'.

Violence

In contrast to peaceful protest, Black Power groups advocated the use of violence in response to racial violence. Malcolm X, for example, argued that black people should seek freedom 'by all means necessary'. Furthermore, he stressed that black people had a constitutional right to own guns and to defend themselves. H. Rapp Brown, who became the head of the SNCC in 1967, also supported the use of violence, urging African Americans to 'get you some guns' and 'kill the honkies'. The Black Panther Party (BPP) — founded by Huey Newton, Bobby Seale and Richard Aoki in 1966 — was another example of black militants who believed that the use of violence was an essential part of the struggle for black rights. The BPP organised an armed self-defence force that 'defended' black communities against the 'foreign occupying force' of racist white police.

Social and economic change

Groups associated with the Black Power movement were advocates of social and economic change. The BPP, for example, had a political platform in the form of the 'Ten-Point Program' which called for, among other things, social and economic equality for black people, the exemption of black citizens from military service, freedom for all black prisoners and an end to racist policing. The programme could be summed up by its first point: 'We want freedom. We want power to determine the destiny of our black community.' Additionally, the BPP created the 'Free Breakfast for

School Children Program', which was providing food for 10,000 children daily by the late 1960s.

Achievements of Black Power

Legal change was never the goal of the Black Power movement. Consequently, the absence of a body of legislation comparable to the Civil Rights Acts and Voting Rights Act cannot be construed as a failure on the movement's part. The Black Power movement certainly had an influence.

First, the emphasis on Black Power and Black Pride encouraged many African Americans to be proud of their racial origins and culture. For example, in the late 1960s the jazz musician Miles Davis started working almost exclusively with other black musicians and deliberately stressed African influences in his musical style. The significance of this point should not be overlooked, for, as Malcolm X argued, 'the worst crime the white man has committed has been to teach us to hate ourselves'.

Secondly, militant groups forced King and other more moderate black leaders to change their focus and address the problems of ghettoisation and the concerns of the northern black underclass. Consequently, King increasingly spoke in terms of Black Pride and about 'revolution' rather than 'reform'.

Thirdly, groups such as the Black Panthers kept the economic position of black Americans on the political agenda through their Ten-Point Program.

Glossary

Nation of Islam: a religious and political organisation founded by Wallace Fard Muhammad in 1930. The organisation preaches a form of Islam that claims that all people were originally black until the artificial creation of white people by an evil scientist. White people are considered to be inferior to black people. Black people are encouraged to have nothing to do with whites and to work hard and live moral lives.

self-determination: the belief that people should be free to govern themselves.

What had the black movement achieved by 1968?

The year 1968 was a turning point for the civil rights campaign, as it witnessed the assassination of Martin Luther King; the election of conservative Richard Nixon as US president; and the imprisonment of Bobby Seale and Huey Newton, co-founders of the Black Panther Party. By 1968, enormous gains had been made, but the majority of African Americans still lived in poverty and faced racial discrimination.

Gains: 1945–68

Politically, the Voting Rights Act (1965) consolidated and extended the gains made by previous campaigns, such as *Smith v Allwright* (1944) and the SNCC's voting registration campaign of 1964 (the Mississippi Freedom Summer). The Act explicitly outlawed any state legislation that barred black people from voting, whatever the pretext. The Act's impact was immediate and significant. By 1968 there were over 3 million registered black voters in the south, and by 1970 1,400 black people had been elected to public office. Moreover, the power of black voters was also evident from the sharp decline of Republican and Democratic candidates in the south who publicly supported segregation. Finally, the state governors in the north responded to the power of black voters by appointing black people to senior positions in their administrations. New York governor Nelson Rockefeller and mayor John V. Lindsay both increased their share of the black vote following the appointment of high-profile black individuals in their administrations.

Similarly, the Civil Rights Act (1964) was the culmination of postwar campaigns for social and economic racial equality. The Act banned segregation across the USA and gave the federal government the power to enforce this ban. By late 1965, 214 cities had formally desegregated and the proportion of black children in segregated schools had decreased substantially. The increased opportunities in education, coupled with the rise of fair employment practices, led to the rise of a black middle class. By 1969 over a third of black households had a combined annual income of $10,000.

The Civil Rights Act (1968) went some way towards ending discrimination in the provision of housing. The Act outlawed any 'Refusal to sell or rent a dwelling to any person because of his race, color, religion or national origin.' It also gave the federal government the power to enforce the Act. Notably, the overwhelming majority of Republican and Democratic members of Congress supported the Act.

Another important change was the increased white support for racial equality between 1945 and 1968, especially in the media. One significant example was the inclusion of a black character, Lieutenant Uhura, in the popular science-fiction series *Star Trek*, as part of the racially mixed crew of the *Starship Enterprise*. Indeed in 1966, the programme featured the first interracial kiss to be screened on US television. The popular prime-time television series *Batman* also cast black actresses and singer Eartha Kitt as Batman and Robin's arch enemy Catwoman in 1967. Similarly, during the 1960s black recording artists, such as Miles Davis, began to insist that black models appeared on their album covers. This trend was also evident in printed media. The *Wall Street Journal*, *Time Magazine* and *The New Yorker* frequently ran articles supporting the campaign for civil rights.

Explaining these achievements

These gains took place for a number of reasons: the successes of the civil rights campaigns; the increasing support of federal government; the impact of the Cold War; sympathy from the Supreme Court; and the involvement of the media.

First, the civil rights campaigns were instrumental in focusing public and government attention on racial inequalities. They also led to the emergence of black leaders who were able to act as figureheads for the black movement, and negotiate with the federal government. This explains the increasing willingness of the federal government to address formal inequalities.

The Kennedy and Johnson administrations were also ideologically committed to ending formal discrimination, and in Johnson's case, his vision of 'The Great Society' also held out the prospect of tackling poverty for all Americans.

Earlier presidents, particularly Truman, saw the paradox of condemning Soviet tyranny and allowing the oppression of African Americans to continue within the USA. Consequently, one effect of the Cold War was to make racial integration a federal issue.

Another factor forcing federal government to address issues of civil rights was Supreme Court rulings. The NAACP was able successfully to demonstrate that segregation was unconstitutional. This reflected a greater liberalism in the Supreme Court's outlook than was evident prior to the Second World War.

Finally, the media played a crucial role in drawing civil rights campaigns to the attention of a wider public, and in increasing support for their goals. Moreover, the media brought figures such as Martin Luther King to national prominence; brought the public's desire for change to the attention of the federal government; and provided further impetus for change by showing the inequity of segregation to a global audience.

The limits of progress by 1968

In spite of the success of the Voting Rights Act (1965), black citizens were still politically marginalised in the USA. A smaller proportion of black people were registered to vote. In northern states, for example, 77% of white voters were registered, whereas only 71% of African-American voters were registered. The situation was worse in the south, where 71% of white Americans were registered, compared to only 62% of black Americans. Furthermore, many southern states elected no black representatives, and many of the appointments made by white politicians in the north were seen as tokenistic. Indeed, the majority of black appointments were made without consulting black voters and those appointed were usually given jobs in race relations. It is also worth noting that in the 1968 presidential election Richard Nixon was elected by appealing to southern white voters rather than attempting to engage black voters.

Progress on social and economic issues was also slow. Black ghettos, with inadequate housing and educational facilities, were still a feature of many northern cities. In 1968, only two northern states had commissions that enforced fair treatment in housing and employment. Similarly, in the south, *de facto* segregation continued, particularly in the areas of education and employment. Indeed, 58% of black children in southern states still attended segregated schools in 1968.

Why was progress limited?

The limits of progress can be explained, in part, by the continuing prejudice of many US whites. The legal changes won by the civil rights movement did not, in and of themselves, weaken the antagonism of racist whites. Racism was not confined to the south. Indeed, the Kerner Commission, established by President Johnson, made this very point when it blamed white racists for the northern ghetto riots. In the south, a number of racist state governors continued to be elected, reflecting ongoing racial prejudice on the part of their white constituents. For example, in 1966, a year after the Voting Rights Act (1965), Lurleen Wallace was elected governor of Alabama due to her commitment to maintain segregated schools. In 1970 her husband, George C. Wallace, was elected for the same reason.

The prejudice of white Americans was not the only factor inhibiting progress. Other factors included the federal government's preoccupation with the Vietnam War, the breakdown of the civil rights coalition in the mid-1960s, the reaction of white opinion to the increasing radicalisation of black campaigners, and the economic nature of the remaining problems.

The escalation of the Vietnam War in 1965 had a major impact on the success of the civil rights movement. First, the war distracted President Johnson from his domestic agenda. Secondly, the war created division between Martin Luther King and President Johnson, following King's criticism of US involvement. Thirdly, the war polarised public opinion, heightening conservatism and nationalism on the right and radicalism on the left.

After 1965, the civil rights movement lost its cohesion. The radicalisation of CORE and the SNCC meant that collaboration between these groups and the SCLC became unviable. These divisions reduced the authority of black leaders, as they could no longer claim to speak for the whole of black America.

Furthermore, the militancy of the Black Panthers, the SNCC and CORE provoked a backlash among white liberals. Consequently, there was no longer a multiracial coalition seeking further integration. Black militancy also provided racist whites with evidence that black people were 'an enemy within' — a point of particular sensitivity as the USA was at war in Vietnam. J. Edgar Hoover, head of the Federal Bureau of Investigation, made this very point when he argued that the Black Panthers were the 'greatest threat to the internal security of the country'.

Finally, Martin Luther King had argued that further change would be more difficult because the remaining problems facing black Americans were economic rather than legal. King suggested that once the emancipation of African Americans started to affect white people financially, they would lose sympathy with the cause. Indeed, the kind of economic change that King's Poor People's Campaign (1968) proposed was opposed by powerful vested interests such as US business.

The 1960s: changing economic and social context

Economic and social context

Prosperity

From 1945 to 1967, the USA enjoyed continuous economic growth. The 1950s and 1960s were a particular time of affluence, and an economic boom in consumer products and housing. The growth of the US economy in the 1950s was astonishing. Gross national product grew from $300,000 million in 1950, to $500,000 million in 1960. The late 1950s and early 1960s also witnessed a change in US working patterns. By 1956, for the first time in the USA's history, the majority of US workers were involved in **white-collar**, rather than **blue-collar**, occupations. What is more, labour unions, which had enjoyed legal recognition since the 1930s, were able to use their power to negotiate increased benefits for workers, such as increased holiday pay and, in some cases, better healthcare. In 1967 President Johnson summed up the success of the postwar economy by stating that the wages of average workers were the highest in US history.

The Great Society

The USA's prosperity was not evenly spread. Significant sections of US society, such as southern farmers, recent immigrants and black Americans, did not enjoy the affluence of the white middle class. President Johnson's 'Great Society' programme attempted to address this problem and distribute wealth more fairly. Johnson acted quickly to deal with inequalities in healthcare provision, housing and urban deprivation. The 1965 Social Security Act provided state-funded healthcare to all Americans who were recipients of state welfare. The Housing and Urban Development Act, also of 1965, committed the government to build 240,000 new homes, as well as establishing a fund of $2.9 billion of government money to be spent on urban renewal. Johnson appointed Robert C. Weaver to oversee this programme. Notably, Weaver was the first African American to be a member of the US cabinet. These provisions were extended under the Fair Housing Act of 1968 (also known as the Civil Rights Act), which outlawed racial discrimination in the property market.

Extending the rights and opportunities of minority groups was an essential part of Johnson's vision of 'The Great Society'. A significant proportion of US citizens on welfare were black. Equally, urban deprivation affected a disproportionate number of African-American citizens. Therefore, Johnson's initiatives targeted some of the important economic problems faced by black people.

Johnson's programmes did not, however, enjoy overwhelming public support. Many white middle-class voters objected to the higher taxes imposed by Johnson to fund welfare benefits for minority groups. Consequently, in the late 1960s, many white voters deserted the Democratic Party and started supporting the more conservative Republicans. This was clearly illustrated in the 1966 congressional elections, where the Republicans made gains in both the Senate and the House of Representatives, taking over 50 congressional seats from the Democrats.

How did economic concerns affect the struggle for civil rights?

Postwar prosperity increased sympathy for the struggle for civil rights. In the 1940s, because of the country's economic problems, white people were concerned that racial equality could only be achieved at their expense. However, in the affluent atmosphere of the 1960s, white people felt more secure and therefore did not fear the prospect of greater racial equality.

Nonetheless, as economic conditions worsened at the end of the 1960s, and as government taxes increased to fund Johnson's 'Great Society', white people began to feel economically stretched and therefore more hostile towards initiatives that benefited other people at their expense. This partly explains Johnson's declining popularity after 1965, as well as decreasing public support for civil rights.

Education

Improving education was another important part of Johnson's vision of the Great Society. Johnson passed two Education Acts to deal with problems at different levels of education. The Elementary and Secondary Education Act of 1965 committed $1.5 billion of government money to improve disadvantaged schools. A great deal of this money went to southern schools that had recently desegregated, and schools in poorer urban areas. The Higher Education Act, also of 1965, provided grants and loans to low-income students, which were designed to enable them to attend US universities. Finally, the Bilingual Education Act of 1968 addressed the problems faced by children who spoke little English, or English as a second language. The government spent $7.5 million over 5 years in order to support bilingual students.

Government education initiatives certainly had a positive effect on students from ethnic minorities. The funds provided by the Higher Education Act led to a fourfold increase in the number of black college students during the late 1960s and early 1970s. The economic benefits of improved access to education for citizens from ethnic minorities were also evident by the end of the 1960s. Approximately 65% of non-white students who had spent 4 years in higher education entered high-paid, professional employment.

Individual teachers also responded to the civil rights campaign. Jane Elliott, for example, devised the famous 'Blue Eyes, Brown Eyes' exercise in response to the assassination of Martin Luther King. Elliott taught in a small town which was almost entirely white. Nonetheless, she was committed to teaching students about the evils of racism. Consequently, in an exercise lasting for 2 days, she first gave privileges to blue-eyed students, claiming there was scientific proof that people with blue eyes were biologically superior. On the second day, she reversed this and favoured the children with brown eyes. The exercise had a profound effect on the children involved, who came to experience the feeling of disempowerment and exclusion. The experiment came to the attention of the national media and influenced public debate on the effects of racial segregation in education.

Mass culture

The US mass media played a part in the civil rights campaigns and also reflected the gains made for black Americans in the 1950s and 1960s. For example, popular prime-time television programmes such as *Batman* and *Star Trek* introduced black actors in leading roles. Additionally, both of these programmes featured episodes that dealt with fictional accounts of racial prejudice.

The government was also involved in trying to make television more representative of the USA at large. In 1967, Congress passed the Public Broadcasting Act. The Act set up the Corporation for Public Broadcasting (CPB), designed to make educational programmes. For example, in 1968, the CPB commissioned a ten-part programme entitled *Black, Blues, Black*, which was written and directed by black poet and writer Maya Angelou. Another show commissioned by the CPB in the late 1960s was *Sesame Street*. The programme is notable for several reasons. First, it contained sequences in both English and Spanish, and therefore was deliberately aimed at Spanish-speaking children. Secondly, many black writers and performers were commissioned to appear on, or provide material for, the show. These included James Brown and the Pointer Sisters.

The civil rights struggle also influenced artists in other media. For example, Harper Lee's prize-winning novel *To Kill a Mockingbird* tells the story of a black man who is falsely accused of raping a white woman in Alabama. The book was published in 1960, and turned into an Oscar-winning film in 1962. Black Power also had a significant impact on US literary culture. Gwendolyn Brooks' collection of poems *In the Mecca* describes life in the Chicago ghetto and was written soon after Brooks, influenced by the Black Power movement, 'rediscovered that she was black'.

The presence of black people in production studios and on the television, which was a consequence of the gains made in the late 1950s and early 1960s, had relatively little effect in the 1960s. However, many of the changes in the media that took place in the late 1960s would affect US culture in the 1970s and 1980s.

Protest culture

Student rebels

Many young people in the 1960s believed that they could create a 'new world' that was different from the world of their parents. The key was political action, often inspired by the civil rights campaign. In the words of the Monkees, the USA's answer to the Beatles, 'We're a new generation and we've got something to say.'

In many ways, teenagers in the 1960s really were a 'new generation'. People who had grown up since the end of the Second World War had never experienced the hardship of the Depression. They had lived in relative prosperity for all of their lives, and were better educated than their parents. Consequently, teenagers and young people in the 1960s were less concerned with their own material wealth and more willing to engage with the wider world. Young people were also more willing to challenge authority. Traditionally, US citizens had respected the government, the army and the justice system. However, the civil rights movement had demonstrated the ways in which government authority had been used unjustly. Many young people, therefore, lost faith in the government and started to believe that the US system was fundamentally flawed.

In the early 1960s, President Kennedy deliberately appealed to young people's enthusiasm and idealism. For example, in 1961 Kennedy established the Peace Corps, which was designed to 'promote world peace and friendship' by sending young volunteers to work in developing countries. By June 1966, 15,000 volunteers had joined the Peace Corps and were working overseas. However, by the late 1960s, interest in the Peace Corps was declining. US involvement in Vietnam had discredited the idea that the US government was interested in promoting peace and friendship with the developing world. Consequently, the government was no longer able to appeal to youthful idealism, and young people looked for alternative organisations through which to campaign for change.

One of the organisations young people turned to was Students for a Democratic Society (SDS). This organisation was formed in 1960 in an attempt to challenge the culture of big business and government power, and in order to reawaken genuine individualism and freedom. Following the lead of civil rights campaigners in the southern states, the SDS organised student sit-ins in 1964 to protect the political rights of students in the University of California at Berkeley.

Another organisation that attracted young radicals was Mario Savio's Free Speech Movement (FSM). Savio was critical of the **bureaucratic** culture that he believed had come to dominate US life. The FSM also organised sit-ins, and although the protests were peaceful, in one notable case it took 600 police officers to remove protesters from university buildings.

Vietnam protest

The USA had been fighting in Vietnam since 1956. However, popular protest against the war started in earnest in the mid-1960s. Anti-war protests formed part of the wider protest culture. In this way, members of the SNCC, the SDS and the FSM all participated in the Vietnam protests. For example, in March 1965, the SDS organised a teach-in at the University of Michigan. During this event — which was attended by both Mario Savio and an SNCC representative — students and staff formed a joint forum to debate and discuss the war in Vietnam.

The government decision to impose a **draft** on US citizens provoked angry protests among students and young people. In Berkeley, California, for example, many burnt their draft cards. The government responded by criminalising the act of burning a draft card in August 1965. However, this did not stop the practice. Indeed, the symbolic burning of draft cards was an important part of a 500,000-strong march in New York in 1967. More radical still was the practice of **self-immolation**. Twenty-two-year-old Roger Allen LaPorte died after setting himself alight outside government buildings in New York in protest at the USA's involvement in Vietnam.

Significantly, the Vietnam War raised troubling racial issues. The Black Panthers described the conflict as a war between a white nation and an Asian nation. Additionally, there was concern about the number of black men who were conscripted into the army and killed fighting 'a white man's war'. Consequently, it is no surprise that many members of groups such as the SNCC were active in the anti-war movement. Indeed, the SNCC arranged a number of anti-war marches in Washington DC. Boxing champion Muhammad Ali also joined the protest, declaring himself a **conscientious objector**. Ali argued that as a Muslim he could not take part in an unjust war. However, he also stated, 'I ain't got no quarrel with them **Viet Cong**...They never called me nigger', which emphasised the common perception that it was white racists, rather than Vietnamese communists, who were the enemy of African Americans. Ali was sentenced to 5 years in prison for his stand against the Vietnam War, although this was later overturned following an appeal.

Women's liberation

The women's movement in the 1960s was inspired by the successes and tactics of the black movement. The SNCC, which had campaigned for racial equality in the early

1960s, turned its attention to women's rights late in 1965. Mary King and Casey Hayden's 'A Kind of Memo' set out the SNCC's new direction. King and Hayden believed that the SNCC's new agenda should be to raise questions about women's rights in such a way that it exposed the deep-rooted injustices that were still present in US society.

The women's movement was divided in similar ways to the civil rights movement. First, there were campaigners who focused on women's political rights. For example, Betty Friedan's *Feminine Mystique* (1963) argued for an end to formal sexual discrimination, particularly in the workplace. Friedan's book, which quickly became a bestseller, led to the establishment of the National Organisation for Women (NOW), which campaigned for a legal end to discrimination, and was to enjoy some success in the early 1970s.

A second faction within the women's movement was more interested in cultural change. For example, Radical Women, founded in 1967, attempted to challenge traditional notions of womanhood. In 1968, Radical Women protested against the Miss America competition by crowning a sheep 'Miss America', auctioning a Miss America dummy, and throwing their underwear, kitchen utensils and cleaning products into a 'freedom trash can'. In the same year, Valerie Solanas founded the Society for Cutting Up Men (SCUM), which published a manifesto calling for the overthrow of the government, an end to money and the complete destruction of all men. Solanas's first target was superstar artist Andy Warhol, whom she attempted to assassinate in 1968. The late 1960s also witnessed the establishment of the Women's International Terrorist Conspiracy from Hell (WITCH), who claimed to have cast spells on prominent men. Finally, radical feminists who aimed at cultural change also embraced lesbianism, arguing that 'feminism in theory is lesbianism in practice'.

Counterculture and individual freedom

The idea of individual freedom united many campaigners for racial equality, sexual equality and an end to the Vietnam War. Many radicals believed that the USA had become dominated by big business, bureaucracy, industry and corrupt politicians. The culture of big business sacrificed individual freedom in order to make money. Bureaucracies treated individuals as if they were numbers, rather than real people. Industries forced people to do boring, repetitive jobs that required no creativity and stifled individuality. Corrupt politicians were more concerned about money than defending the rights of individuals.

Many young people who felt alienated by US culture began lifestyle experiments which became known as the counterculture. The desire for individual freedom was central to this cultural experimentation. The best-known examples of 1960s counterculture were the hippies. Hippy style, with its long hair, flared jeans, tie-dyed shirts and sandals, was a clear rejection of conservative business culture, which emphasised traditional dress. Rather than engaging with contemporary culture, hippies were happy to 'drop out' — that is to say, to reject the values of modern life and search for alternatives. One important alternative was **LSD**, a hallucinogenic drug that hippies used to 'expand their consciousness'. The counterculture also took the form of rural communes in which hippies attempted to live at one with each other and at one with nature. In theory, the commune was a place in which people could express their true individuality rather than being forced to conform to socially acceptable roles.

Notably, although the counterculture was inspired by the civil rights movement, the majority of people involved were white, middle class and college educated. Equally, the people who were involved with the counterculture were no longer involved in protest. Their aim was to establish a new culture rather than reforming the existing culture.

Other racial minorities

Native Americans

The 1960s witnessed the emergence of a campaign for Native American rights. Inspired by the gains of the civil rights movement, Native Americans began to draw attention to the disadvantages that their community was forced to suffer. For example, the Native American community had lower life expectancy, a higher suicide rate and a higher unemployment rate than white Americans. Furthermore, they believed that they, like US blacks, were the victims of historic injustices. Indeed, their adoption of the name 'Native Americans', rather than 'American Indians', drew attention to the fact that the USA had originally been their homeland alone, and that they had never been compensated for the land that they had lost following European colonisation.

In 1965 and 1968, President Johnson used federal power to try and help Native Americans. In 1965, Johnson established the National Advisory Council on Indian Education to increase literacy rates among Native Americans. In 1968, he formed the National Council on Indian Opportunity, which — as part of the Great Society programme — was designed to alleviate poverty within Native American communities. In addition, his 1968 Housing Act, also known as the 1968 Civil Rights Act, outlawed discrimination against Native Americans in the housing market.

However, Johnson's initiatives were considered inadequate by Native American radicals, who started a direct action campaign in the style of the Black Power movement. The American Indian Movement (AIM) was established in 1968 in order to promote 'red power'. Similar to the Black Power movement, AIM advocated Native American pride. It was also similar to the Black Panthers in the sense that it was suspicious of the police and sought to protect the Native American community from police harassment. AIM's radicalism was not restricted to the Native American community. Indeed, AIM was instrumental in the establishment of the women's rights group NOW.

Hispanic Americans

Hispanic Americans were another minority group who faced persecution and discrimination within the USA. Like Black Americans, they had poorer educational opportunities, often lived in urban ghettos and earned less than their white counterparts. Indeed, in 1961, the average Hispanic American income was approximately a third less than that of white Americans. What is more, Hispanic Americans were often stereotyped as ignorant and work-shy.

The Democratic administrations of Presidents Kennedy and Johnson took some small steps towards racial equality, which had a direct effect on the Hispanic community. In 1963 Kennedy proposed the abolition of quotas in the US immigration system. Since the 1920s, immigration to the USA had been restricted through a series of quotas that specified the proportion of immigrants that were allowed to enter the country from various ethnic groups. This system explicitly favoured immigrants from northwest Europe. The system was devised to ensure that white Anglo-Saxon culture would remain dominant. Kennedy recognised the injustice of this system and, following his death, his successor, President Johnson, passed the 1965 Immigration Act, which abolished these prejudicial quotas. The Act removed caps on Hispanic immigrants from Europe, Latin America and Mexico.

Hispanic American activists, like Native Americans and feminists, adopted the methods that had been pioneered by civil rights campaigners. Like Native Americans and African Americans involved with the Black Power movement, many Hispanic activists were keen to demonstrate their pride in their ethnic identity. Consequently, they began to use the term 'Chicano' to describe themselves. Originally, Chicano had been a term of abuse, primarily directed at Mexicans. However, Hispanic activists reinvented the term as a highly positive description which encompassed Mexicans, Spanish Americans and immigrants from Latin America.

Hispanic radicals also engaged in direct action. For example, Hispanic activist Sal Castro organised the 1968 Chicano Blowouts, a series of strikes in Los Angeles which were part of a campaign designed to highlight inequalities in the US education system. Many of the students who took part in the Blowouts, however, were more concerned about the rising death toll of Hispanic soldiers in the Vietnam War.

Perhaps the best-known Hispanic activist was César Chavez, who founded the Untied Farm Workers (UFW) in 1962. Chavez's organisation represented immigrant farm workers who were not protected by the National Labour Relations Act of 1935 and therefore did not qualify for the legal minimum wage. Chavez was clearly influenced by the example of Martin Luther King. Both leaders were committed Christians and, because of this, favoured non-violent protest. Chavez's high-profile campaigns, including a national grape boycott and a personal fast, gained media attention and, although there was no legal change prior to 1970, Chavez gained the sympathy of prominent politicians such as Senator Robert F. Kennedy.

Glossary

blue collar: describes a working-class occupation based on manual labour, such as factory work.

bureaucratic: a system of administration or management where administrative work is delegated to a large number of officials. In practice, this is often a derogatory term used to describe a system in which paperwork has become more important than human beings.

conscientious objector: an individual who refuses to engage in military service for moral or religious reasons.

draft: in this context, the conscription of men to fight for the US army. During the Vietnam War, those who had been conscripted received a 'draft card' calling them up to fight.

LSD: a hallucinogenic recreational drug, sometimes known as acid.

self-immolation: the act of setting fire to oneself as a form of protest.

Viet Cong: the guerrilla army that fought the USA and the South Vietnamese armies during the Vietnam War.

white collar: describes a middle-class professional occupation.

Questions
&
Answers

This section contains five specimen exam questions. Two specimen answers are given to each question: an A-grade and a C-grade response. All the specimen answers are the subject of detailed examiner comments, preceded by the icon ℮. These should be studied carefully because they show how and why marks are awarded or lost.

When exam papers are marked, all answers are given a level of response and then a precise numerical mark. Answers are normally marked accordingly to five levels:

- **level 1**: 1–6 marks
- **level 2**: 7–12 marks
- **level 3**: 13–18 marks
- **level 4**: 19–24 marks
- **level 5**: 25–30 marks

Question 1

Why was progress towards racial equality so slow in the years 1945–55? (30 marks)

■ ■ ■

A-grade answer

Progress towards racial equality was slow between 1945 and 1955 for a number of reasons. These include the lack of wholehearted support from federal government, the absence of organised protest, the lack of a spokesman for black people, the limits of the NAACP's campaign, public opinion and the absence of media attention. Media attention was perhaps the most crucial factor in the success of the civil rights campaigns of the 1960s, and therefore it is clear that the lack of media attention in the decade following the Second World War was the single biggest reason for slow progress towards racial equality.

> This is a focused introduction that outlines the structure of the rest of the essay, and states the overall judgement that the lack of media attention was the key reason for slow progress during this decade.

Between 1945 and 1955 US Presidents Truman and Eisenhower were either unsympathetic to, or distracted from, advancing civil rights. Although Truman brought in a number of measures to help African Americans (like desegregating the army) he also knew that his party was dependent on the votes of racist whites in the south. Additionally, the end of his presidency was spent dealing with the Korean War, which distracted him from further moves towards desegregation. Eisenhower, on the other hand, was unsympathetic to the plight of black people. He thought that black people were aggressive and ungrateful for their position in the USA and therefore he failed to enforce the Brown decision of 1954. Without federal support it was very difficult for civil rights campaigners to achieve their goals as federal government was the only agency able to effect civil rights policy across the whole of the USA.

> This makes a clear point, backs it up with specific examples and finally explains its relevance to the question. This is an excellent structure replicated throughout the essay.

Also between 1945 and 1955 there was no coherent mass protest. In the 1960s the movement achieved notable success, challenging Jim Crow laws using high-profile and organised mass campaigns. For example, the Birmingham campaign of 1963 achieved some success in challenging segregation in public places. In the late 1940s and early 1950s, however, challenges to segregation were mostly legal. Examples of this are the NAACP's case challenging segregation in interstate travel, *Morgan* v *Virginia* (1946), and the Brown case of 1954 challenging segregation in schools. These campaigns were slow to advance the cause of racial equality because they did not attract the kind of media attention that mass action would a decade later.

question

The campaign was also slow due to the lack of a black figurehead. The absence of a figure like Martin Luther King meant that there was nobody to speak to the media or to federal government on behalf of the black community. Equally, there was no unifying figure to rally black support to the fight against Jim Crow. Later campaigns, such as the 1963 March on Washington, owed much of their success to the leadership of Martin Luther King. His speaking abilities and capacity to unify were shown to great effect in this campaign, where he delivered his 'I have a dream' speech to a mixed-race crowd of over 250,000 people. The absence of a charismatic leader slowed progress as mass black dissatisfaction could not be organised and channelled into mass campaigns for change.

Throughout this period the racism of many whites remained unchanged. Groups such as the KKK influenced opinion in the south. In the north the existence of black ghettos prevented racial integration and therefore hindered acceptance of African Americans as equals. Progress was slow because there simply wasn't the public support which was clearly necessary before change could happen.

Finally, the NAACP's focus on legal change, the absence of a charismatic black leader, and the fact that the media were dominated by whites meant that the media were not interested in the struggle for equality during this period. For example, despite its importance, the Brown case failed to attract substantial media coverage, which meant that the majority of Americans remained ignorant of the injustices of segregation and the anti-segregation campaign. The absence of media coverage explains the limited progress towards equality as without publicity it was difficult to increase support.

> The beginning of this paragraph demonstrates how the different factors discussed in the essay interlink. This substantiated explanation ensures that the essay is awarded a high mark.

In essence, progress was slow between 1945 and 1955 because the campaigns of this period lacked many of the characteristics that made later campaigns so successful. Without federal support, a charismatic leader and the development of mass protest, the movement was unable to gain media attention. After 1955, this media attention proved crucial in gaining public support and ensuring legal change. For this reason, the absence of media attention can be seen as the most important reason for the slow pace of change between 1945 and 1955.

> **This is a fine essay. The factors discussed demonstrate detailed knowledge of a range of different issues. The explanatory focus on the question is rock solid throughout. In addition, the candidate clearly understands the way in which the factors combined to produce the end result, and uses this information to reach a judgement about the relative importance of these factors.**

Level 5: 30/30

■ ■ ■

C-grade answer

Many African Americans faced discrimination and racial inequality in 1945. In the south there was legal discrimination through Jim Crow laws, such as grandfather clauses, and in the north many African Americans lived in ghettos with bad housing. The government supported this to an extent and segregated the army with black people having one mess hall and white people having another. So in 1945 the position of black people was bad and they needed a lot of progress.

📝 The introduction simply describes the background to the question. It does not really address the question.

The NAACP was a group that helped to fight these problems such as the Jim Crow laws. It used legal methods and took the government to court over education and transport to try and get some change. But this was a very slow process as the courts were not sympathetic to black issues as few judges were black. Also the court cases took a long time because there were lots of courts before they got to the Supreme Court which made the final decision. Even when they did make a decision, sometimes it was vague so they had to fight the case all over again. For example, in the Brown case the court decided that Linda Brown could go to a white school because she lived really close to it. But because the judges didn't say when the schools should let black people in, they had to go to court again. This case was called Brown II.

📝 The focus of the second paragraph is better, and it does contain some specific information (the reference to the Brown case).

The presidents were also not much help. Truman desegregated the armed forces and set up a report called *To Secure These Rights*. The report showed that there was a lot of progress to be made before black people were equal to white people. The report was a ten-point programme which upset a lot of white politicians because they were racist. President Eisenhower's acts were not very helpful. He passed a Civil Rights Act in 1960 but it was also opposed by important white politicians so it was not very effective when it was passed because they changed it.

📝 Again, there is some specific support within this paragraph. However, the information about President Eisenhower cannot be credited as it is outside the period stated in the question.

White people were still very racist and they did not want change. Many people in important positions were racists. The Ku Klux Klan still had a lot of power and tried to stop change happening. They were very successful and this explains why the change was very slow between 1945 and 1955.

📝 Although this contains an explanatory link to the question, the lack of supporting evidence makes it little more than an unsubstantiated assertion.

Many black people did not have the vote in the south because of grandfather clauses. These were where black people could not vote until they had a grandfather who had voted. Most black grandfathers had been slaves and so could not vote. Also, black people were asked impossible questions like 'how many bubbles are there in a bar of soap?' This meant that they could not vote for change, so change was slow in the years 1945 to 1955. This kept black people out of power and so white racists like the KKK could run the government in the south.

> This paragraph does attempt to make a direct link to the question. It explains why denying black people the vote led to slow progress in achieving racial equality.

Because black people had worse education than white people, they were not able to get into good jobs or positions of power. So there were few black people in the media and so the media were not interested in black problems. Lack of media interest meant that progress was slow towards racial equality in the years 1945 to 1955 to an extent.

So the progress was slow due to many factors like white racism and the grandfather clauses.

> The conclusion is extremely weak. It does not really summarise the points made in the essay.

> **This answer focuses on the question throughout. It also discusses a range of factors. However, there are weaknesses within the essay. For example, only one of the paragraphs contains an explanatory link to the question. Moreover, much of the essay is either vague or simplistic. Nonetheless, there is sufficient specific detail to ensure that the essay achieves high level 3.**

Level 3: 17/30

Question 2

How far do you agree that the failure of Martin Luther King's northern campaigns was the main reason for increased militancy among black protesters? (30 marks)

■ ■ ■

A-grade answer

Militancy increased among black protesters in the 1960s for a variety of reasons, such as the failure of Martin Luther King's northern campaigns, increasing frustration with the pace of change, the emergence of radical alternatives to peaceful protest, wider social trends such as the emergence of a protest culture, and the economic problems of many blacks. Although King's failures contributed to increased radicalisation, they cannot be considered the major factor because radicalism was growing in the early 1960s at a time when King was enjoying considerable success.

King's northern campaigns were not as successful as his campaigns in the southern states, and this undoubtedly caused some black people to embrace more militant forms of protest. For African Americans the failure of the Chicago campaign of 1966 indicated that King's methods and tactics were no longer effective. Additionally, King's Christian rhetoric was out of step with the culture of northern African Americans and in many ways King's southern middle-class upbringing meant that he did not understand the racial problems in the north. For example, King had little experience of urban deprivation and the violent culture of the ghettos. Consequently, King's increasing marginalisation led to a movement away from his non-violent philosophy and as a result support for militant alternatives increased.

☞ This essay begins by focusing on the factor stated in the question. This is a good technique, as it ensures that the question has been properly dealt with before there is any danger of running out of time.

However, even before King's move to the north, many black Americans were impatient with the rate of reform. Following the 1964 Civil Rights Act and the 1965 Voting Rights Act the pace of change slowed. This was for a number of reasons. Primarily, the government felt that in overturning Jim Crow with the Civil Rights Act and the Voting Rights Act they had met the demands of black campaigners. These acts abolished segregation and ensured political equality for black citizens. Additionally, the Vietnam War distracted President Johnson, diverting both money and attention away from domestic issues. Clearly, militancy was increasing prior to King's failure in the north, and therefore this should not be considered the most important reason for the rise of more radical alternatives.

☞ The final sentence is a good example of an explanatory link and evaluation. The sentence offers a counter-argument which shows that Martin Luther King's failure in the north was not the primary reason for increased militancy.

Another reason for increasing militancy was the emergence of charismatic leaders in the Black Power movement. Malcolm X, for example, was a leading figure who argued that black people had the right to defend themselves. He also described King's 'dream' as a 'nightmare', suggesting that integration would lead to greater enslavement of the black community. Stokely Carmichael also appealed to more radical desires with his phrase 'Black Power'. He suggested militant methods, such as burning down government property, which clearly appealed to impoverished northern blacks who believed that the white government was deliberately oppressing them. Finally, the Black Panther Party's Ten-Point Programme offered the hope of increased welfare and better jobs for black people. Each of these alternatives addressed the needs of blacks in urban ghettos, and therefore attracted growing support. Indeed, this radical message had gained significant support by the mid-1960s, which suggests that militancy had considerable appeal even before King's failure in the north.

The increasing support for militancy can also be seen as part of a wider social trend. The rise of Black Power was an expression of the wider protest culture which was popular with young people throughout the 1960s. Women were radicalised and joined groups such as PIG (Politically Interested Girlies); students joined Marxist groups and organised sit-ins. Similarly, young black people became radicalised and joined the Black Panthers or SNCC. This protest culture was originally inspired by the success of Martin Luther King's peaceful protest in the early 1960s. Therefore, it is possible to argue that it was King's early success — rather than his later failure — which led to the generation of the 1960s protest culture of which black militancy was a part.

Essentially it was the scale and nature of the problems facing African Americans after 1965 that best explains the turn to militancy. Social and economic problems such as northern ghettos, *de facto* discrimination in the workplace, and widespread black poverty could not simply be solved by passing laws. Had it been possible to solve the problems of the north with legislation alone, it is arguable that Johnson would have taken steps to achieve this, King's methods would have been more appropriate and militant protest would have seemed disproportional. Militancy was not a first choice for many black Americans but by the late 1960s it had become a last resort.

> **This answer does everything it should. It discusses five factors in some detail, and it is packed with explanatory and evaluative links to the question. Additionally, the answer contains a number of sophisticated points which show knowledge of the change in American culture over time.**
>
> **Level 5: 30/30**

■ ■ ■

C-grade answer

In the early days of the civil rights movement it was not very militant at all. But when Martin Luther King failed in his northern campaigns, the black civil rights movement was much more militant. This was also because of Malcolm X and the Black Panthers.

Lots of people were disappointed with Martin Luther King's northern campaigns. They had expected him to go to the north and solve all of their problems like he had in the south. But when he got to the north he realised that he did not really know about the problems in the north. He did not know that northern people were so racist. Because of this his campaigns failed. In Chicago, the mayor (a man called Richard Daley) made lots of promises that he did not keep and so King stopped the campaign even though it had not achieved anything. He looked like a 'white man's tool'. When lots of black people saw that Martin Luther King had failed, they decided that they needed a new leader and that man was Malcolm X. Even though he was dead, people still believed in his ideas and began to use violent protest.

Malcolm X was a very radical and militant black nationalist freedom fighter. In a famous picture he is seen holding a shotgun and looking out of the window. Malcolm X's father was able to build his own house and business. But the KKK burned his house down in 1929, and later murdered him when Malcolm X was six. Malcolm X taught that black people should fight back, 'an eye for an eye'. His father was a Baptist preacher, but Malcolm X was a Muslim and he did not believe in the Christian message of 'turning the other cheek'. Malcolm X was not in favour of desegregation like Martin Luther King, as he went to a mixed school that was run by whites. His English teacher told him to become a carpenter not a lawyer so he dropped out of school and he could see that white teachers did not encourage black children. When he moved to Harlem he was nicknamed 'Detroit Red' and he sold drugs and became a pimp. When he was caught he was sentenced to 10 years. This was racist because he was a first-time offender and it made him very militant. In prison he wanted to be free from prison but also from white people's power. He turned to the Nation of Islam where he became a Muslim. The Nation of Islam said that white people were evil and would make black people slaves. This made Malcolm X very militant against white people.

📝 This paragraph demonstrates considerable knowledge of Malcolm X's biography. However, most of the information is not targeted at the question.

Malcolm X had lots of followers. In 1964 Malcolm X toured American universities giving a speech called 'Ballot or the bullet'. The speech persuaded many American students to support his ideas. He called King 'Uncle Tom', which meant that he would not stand up to the white man. This increased the militancy of the movement because like him they believed that there could be no freedom under white people.

📝 Here the candidate makes a point and then links it to the question with some relevant development.

The Black Panthers were militant as well as Malcolm X. They had a Ten-Point Programme. Their programme was militant because it wanted to release all black people from prison, even murderers and rapists. They said that all black prisoners were political prisoners and the police were racists. They believed that the police were fascist and racist and they could fight them. They organised a defence force to protect black people from racist attacks from white police and the KKK. The Black Panthers became very popular because one of their leaders was the victim of police racism.

question

One of the first Black Panthers, Bobby Seale, protested about racism and he was locked up by the police for this protest. Huey Newton was another Black Panther who used militant methods. He was arrested for killing a white policeman. This made the Panthers more popular because the 'Free Huey' campaign struck a chord with northern African Americans and gave a focus to the Panthers' activities. Because groups like the Black Panthers offered black Americans what they wanted, they became more popular and Martin Luther King's failure wasn't really the reason for this.

This paragraph makes a clear and relevant point, followed by adequate development, and concludes with a clear link back to the question.

The Black Panthers and Malcolm X had a big influence and people became more militant. The film *Shaft* shows a group of Black Panthers fighting the mafia using militant methods. *Shaft* was very popular and made black power look very exciting and glamorous, as did *Sweet Sweetback's Badass Song* which also made the Panthers heroes. King didn't look as heroic after his failures in the north.

Strictly speaking Shaft *and* Sweet Sweetback's Baadasssss Song *were released in 1971, so they are not relevant examples as the question asks about the late 1960s.*

Black militancy was more popular because of important figures and groups like the Black Panthers and Malcolm X, who had lots of followers who spread their militant ideas, not because Martin Luther King failed in the north.

Essentially this answer states that militancy grew because Malcolm X and the Black Panthers grew in popularity. It also attempts to explain Malcolm X's militancy in terms of his personal history. It is full of accurate details. However, many of these details do not address the question. For example, the fact that he was nicknamed 'Detroit Red' is irrelevant to the question set. Better selection would have helped this essay to answer the question. Nonetheless, it scrapes into level 4 due to the fact that the first paragraph has a clear focus on the question and contains specific supporting information. Additionally, there is some attempt to analyse the reasons for increasing militancy, although this would need to be further developed for the essay to get a higher mark within level 4.

Level 4: 19/30

Question 3

How far had racial equality been achieved in the USA by 1968? (30 marks)

■ ■ ■

A-grade answer

By 1968, racial equality had been broadly achieved in terms of political rights, but there was still a long way to go in social, economic and cultural terms. It should be remembered that racial equality is not just about blacks and whites, as in this context it also relates to Native Americans and Hispanic Americans.

By 1968, significant progress had been made in terms of political rights. Importantly, the 1965 Voting Rights Act was the culmination of campaigns such as *Smith* v *Allwright* (1944), Eisenhower's Civil Rights Acts of 1957 and 1960, and SNCC's Mississippi Freedom Summer of 1964. The Act made it illegal to deny black people the vote in any circumstances. Therefore, grandfather clauses and literacy tests were finally outlawed. By 1968, over 3 million black people had been added to the electoral register in southern states, and over a thousand black people had been elected to public office. Clearly, a great deal of progress had been made towards achieving racial equality in political rights by 1968 because, for the first time, the government had passed a definitive Act to ensure the rights of black people.

However, there were still ways in which blacks and whites were politically unequal. This inequality was particularly pronounced in the southern states. For example, by 1965, while 71% of southern whites were registered to vote, only 62% of blacks in the south were on the electoral register. What is more, as late as 1966, 4 out of 13 southern states still had fewer than 50% of blacks registered to vote. In this way, although blacks had the same *de jure* rights as whites, their *de facto* position, particularly in the south, was still very much that of a second-class citizen.

> The previous two paragraphs set out the case for and against the achievement of racial equality in terms of political rights. This is an effective way of organising the information. Additionally, they end with a mini-conclusion that evaluates this aspect of racial equality.

In terms of social and economic rights, some equality had been achieved by 1968. The 1964 Civil Rights Act, for example, finally banned segregation across the USA. This had an immediate effect on racial equality. By late 1965, 214 cities had desegregated. Additionally, the proportion of black children in segregated schools substantially decreased. The Fair Employment Practices Commission also encouraged the rise of a new black middle class, and therefore during the 1960s, black income doubled. Therefore, it is fair to say that there was some progress towards racial equality in social and economic terms due to the provisions of President Johnson's civil rights legislation.

Again, racial equality was not wholly achieved by 1968. First, 58% of black schoolchildren remained in segregated schools in 1968. Secondly, 7% of blacks were unemployed, whereas the national rate of unemployment was only 5%. Finally, even though black income had risen in the 1960s, the average black family still only earned 61% of the average white family. For this reason, racial equality was only partially achieved in social and economic terms because black people were still disadvantaged in terms of employment, education and income.

> This paragraph makes excellent use of statistics to illustrate the extent to which social and economic equality had been achieved by 1968.

The portrayal of blacks in the media undoubtedly changed during this period. For example, television companies began to cast black actors in leading roles. *Batman and Robin* featured a black actress as Catwoman, and *Star Trek* also broke new ground because it included the first interracial kiss shown on American TV. In music too, black artists such as Miles Davis and Jimmy Hendrix were heavily promoted. However, it was still acceptable to create television programmes which featured no black characters at all, such as *Scooby Doo*, which was first screened in 1968. Indeed, all-white casts and stereotypical presentations of racial minorities remained normal for much of the 1960s, and therefore racial equality in the media had not been fully achieved by 1968.

Native Americans and Hispanic Americans still suffered from racial discrimination by 1968. They had both benefited from President Johnson's civil rights legislation, and both communities had active civil rights campaigns. However, immigrant Hispanic farm workers still did not qualify for the minimum wage. In many ways, racial minorities such as Native Americans and Hispanic Americans were still the victims of prejudice in spite of the gains of the civil rights movement in the 1960s.

In conclusion, racial equality had only been achieved to a limited extent by 1968. Although significant progress had been made since 1945 — both formally and in *de facto* terms — blacks, Native Americans and Hispanic Americans all still suffered from discrimination in terms of economic opportunities, educational provision and their portrayal in the media. The greatest gains were made in political rights, thanks to the Voting Rights Act of 1965, but even here minorities, particularly in the south, were still at a disadvantage in 1968.

> This conclusion evaluates the evidence and presents a summary of the argument of the essay, with a clear focus on 'how far' equality had been achieved. For this reason, the essay meets the requirements of the question and is awarded a higher mark than more simplistic essays which essentially offer a 'yes or no' answer.

> **This is a very strong essay that focuses on the question from beginning to end. It makes excellent use of specific information and statistics to support its points. It is also wide ranging and considers political, social, economic and cultural aspects of the question. In each case, the essay evaluates the extent to which equality had been achieved. The essay also considers other**

racial minorities and therefore answers the question in the fullest sense. Nonetheless, the paragraph dealing with **Native Americans and Hispanic Americans** contains quite limited supporting information.

Level 5: 27/30

■ ■ ■

C-grade answer

Black and white people were clearly equal in 1968 and this was the first time in the history of the USA that this was true. I will show this by considering the Civil Rights Acts of 1964 and 1968 and the Voting Rights Act of 1965 and the success of Martin Luther King's campaigns.

ⓔ The introduction clearly answers the question, but is far too one-sided. This suggests that the rest of the essay will be equally unbalanced.

The Civil Rights Acts helped to achieve equality for blacks in the following ways. It banned segregation which meant that black people could sit on buses on the same seats as white people. It also made sure that black people and white people could shop in the same places, go to the same libraries, and eat in the same restaurants. This was very important in the south where Jim Crow laws had historically meant that black people were second-class citizens and had to give up their seats to white people on buses, even though black people used the buses more.

Another Act which helped to achieve racial equality by 1968 was the 1968 Civil Rights Act passed by President Johnson. This Act ensured that the state had power to prevent any discrimination over the buying, selling and renting of houses. This was very important for black people in the north, who lived in ghettos where the housing was inadequate. In 1968, this was very successful because two northern states set up commissions to enforce fair treatment in the housing market for black people. These Acts were very helpful because one achieved equality in the south by ending segregation, and the other achieved equality in the north by ending discrimination in the ghettos.

The Voting Rights Act played a big part in achieving racial equality because it meant that whites and blacks had the same right to vote. Many blacks registered to vote in the southern states and by 1965, 6 million blacks were voters, compared to 4 million in 1960. Also, the mayor of Gary, Indiana, and the mayor of Cleveland were both black. The Voting Rights Act can be seen as a very important step in achieving racial equality by 1968 because it outlawed grandfather clauses and other cunning means of denying black people the vote.

ⓔ The three paragraphs above only consider the progress that had been made, and do not offer a balanced treatment of the topic.

One reason racial equality was achieved was the leadership of Martin Luther King. Despite being a black man living in the south, he was well educated and able to make powerful speeches. During the Montgomery bus boycott of 1955–56, he organised a 50,000-strong protest and encouraged the churches to fight for civil rights. The Birmingham campaign of 1963 showed the power of peaceful protest in the face of police brutality and water cannon. King's campaign got the media interested in racial equality. The March on Washington also persuaded the government to take civil rights seriously and 250,000 marchers listened to King's 'I have a dream' speech. King's efforts helped achieve equality, as his campaigns led to desegregation and were an important reason for the passing of the Civil Rights Acts.

> *e* This paragraph has some focus on the question, but essentially just tells the story of King's most successful campaigns. Nonetheless, the final sentence clearly answers the question and links King's campaigns to the achievements that have been discussed in the previous paragraphs.

Overall, racial equality had been achieved by 1968 as the Voting Rights Act gave political equality to blacks while the Civil Rights Act guaranteed an end to segregation. These Acts helped black people in the north and the south.

> *e* **The biggest problem with this answer is the fact that it is extremely one-sided. Therefore, it does not truly answer the question because it does not consider 'how far' equality had been achieved. Nonetheless, there is a significant amount of specific detail, a clear focus on the issue raised by the question, and a real attempt to show how the information discussed is relevant to the question.**

Level 4: 19/30

Question 4

How significant was the Vietnam War in stimulating the protest culture of the 1960s?

(30 marks)

■ ■ ■

A-grade answer

The Vietnam War was very significant in stimulating the protest culture of the 1960s, but there were also other important factors.

☑ This introduction is focused, but extremely weak. This is one of the reasons that the answer remains in level 4.

Student protest also encouraged the protest culture. Teenagers in the 1960s believed that they were a new generation. They wanted to change the world and make it a better place. There were the Students for a Democratic Society (SDS) who organised sit-ins. In this way, student protest led to the protest culture because it encouraged young people to believe that they could make the world a better place through protest.

Women were also active in the protest culture in the 1960s. In 1963, a woman called Betty Friedan published a book called *The Feminine Mystique*. The book demanded the ending of discrimination in the workplace. The book was very influential and soon NOW (National Organisation for Women) was set up. Other organisations included RW (Radical Women) and SCUM (Society for Cutting Up Men). SCUM targeted Andy Warhol, whereas RW attacked the Miss America Pageant. RW also organised the 'Freedom Trash Can' and encouraged women to put their bras into it. Also, radical feminists became lesbians, believing that all contact with men was essentially bad. The women's movement was another important cause of the protest culture because women believed that protest was the only way to achieve sexual equality.

☑ The two paragraphs dealing with student protest and women's rights are unbalanced. The essay says practically nothing about student protest, but contains a great deal of information about women's rights.

There are many examples of the counterculture in the 1960s. For the first time since the Second World War, people decided to 'drop out'. They became hippies and took LSD. They rejected big business, consumerism and corrupt politics. Many hippies were really middle class and were rejecting the values of their parents. Hippies sometimes lived in communes, rather than getting married and living in suburbia.

☑ The information in this paragraph is accurate, but the answer does not demonstrate why it is relevant to the question.

Another reason for the 1960s protest culture was the Vietnam War. Young people objected to the draft which forced American citizens to fight in Vietnam. Burning draft cards was an important part of the protest, and continued to be an important symbol

of the anti-war movement even after it was outlawed. Many black people felt that Vietnam was a 'white man's war'. Muhammad Ali was very famous at the time and made lots of people think about the war when he said that the Viet Cong had never treated black people badly. The Vietnam War was another important reason for the protest culture because young people, black people and peace activists could unite in a common cause and therefore increase the scale of the protest.

The civil rights movement was also an important reason for the protest culture. Campaigns such as the Montgomery bus boycott in 1955–56 and the Greensboro sit-ins in 1960 proved that protest worked. In both cases, the protesters got what they wanted. Malcolm X was also influential because he became a powerful symbol for discontent. The success of the civil rights movement persuaded women's rights campaigners, peace campaigners and student radicals that protest was effective and therefore I would say that the civil rights movement was the most important cause of the protest culture.

🖉 The final two paragraphs are detailed and focused. What is more, the very last paragraph contains a clear and well-presented argument which evaluates the significance of the civil rights movement and reaches a supported judgement.

🖉 **This essay contains three extremely good paragraphs. However, two of the paragraphs are rather weak. This lack of balance, the descriptive nature of the paragraph on counter-culture, and the weakness of the development of student protest keeps the mark within level 4.**

Level 4: 24/30

■ ■ ■

C-grade answer

There were many causes of the protest culture of the 1960s, other than Vietnam.

Prosperity was one of the reasons for the protest culture. In the 1940s and 1950s people were still feeling the effects of the Great Depression. Their focus was on working hard and staying out of poverty. By the 1960s, the economy was much better and many people were much richer. Therefore, many young people had a different point of view from their parents. They were not worried about being in debt or struggling to get a job. They wanted to make a fairer society. They were also critical of big business and the mass media and wanted individual freedom. Mario Savio was a figurehead for this movement and organised sit-ins.

The mass media was also a factor which increased protest. Books like *To Kill a Mockingbird* made people believe that racism was wrong. Also, television coverage of the Watts Riots and the Birmingham campaign made everyone realise that change was necessary in America. They showed how important protest could be in making changes. Malcolm X also became a media figure and therefore his message of protest was spread very widely.

Students were very radical and were quick to protest, leading to a greater protest culture in the 1960s. Students for a Democratic Society (SDS) encouraged students to protest in order to advance individual freedom. There were sit-ins to protect the rights of students in California in 1964. Also, the Free Speech Movement (FSM) organised sit-ins that had to be dealt with by 600 police.

Vietnam was another factor that made protest more radical in the 1960s. The Vietnam War had started in 1956, and by 1960 there was already a protest movement. The protest movement attracted members from other groups like SNCC, SDS and FSM. SDS organised a teach-in at the University of Michigan as a form of protest. Other forms of protest included self-immolation, which means setting yourself on fire. One final form of protest was to be a conscientious objector.

Civil rights was another factor which increased protest. The civil rights movement demonstrated that protest could work. The March on Washington of 1963 led to the Civil Rights Act of 1964 and the Voting Rights Act of 1965 which made America much fairer. Native Americans set up the American Indian Movement (AIM) to try and achieve the same thing. Hispanic Americans, led by Chavez, set up United Farm Workers in 1962. Chavez was very influenced by Martin Luther King.

The protest culture in the 1960s was caused by a number of factors, such as the civil rights movement, new student movements, the mass media and the Vietnam War. Prosperity was also another factor.

This essay contains a wide range of detailed knowledge, organised into appropriate paragraphs, each dealing with a different relevant factor. However, at no point does it explicitly explain the way in which the factors it discusses caused the protest culture of the 1960s. For this reason, the essay is awarded a mark at the top of level 3. To access the higher levels, some explicit explanation is necessary.

Level 3: 18/30

Question 5

Why was the Civil Rights Act of 1964 passed?   (30 marks)

■ ■ ■

A-grade answer

The 1964 Civil Rights Act is often seen as the climax of the postwar civil rights campaigns. It would not have come about had it not been for the unity of the civil rights movement and the March on Washington, as well as the sympathetic media and public. Individuals also had their roles to play — these include Kennedy, Johnson and Martin Luther King.

e The opening demonstrates an understanding of the importance of the topic. Furthermore, it outlines a thematic approach to the question. However, it does not state which of the factors is most important and therefore misses an opportunity to evaluate the causes of the Civil Rights Act.

The early 1960s witnessed a significant degree of unity between different civil rights groups. At this time, the SCLC, SNCC, CORE and the NAACP were all committed to integration through non-violent means. For example, SCLC emerged out of the Montgomery bus boycott of 1955–56 and SNCC out of the spontaneous sit-ins in Greensboro in 1960. This unity of aims and methods, coupled with the successes of these non-violent protests, led to the passing of the Civil Rights Act in 1964 because it showed the strength of support for civil rights issues and therefore forced politicians to take civil rights issues seriously.

Popular support was crucial to the passing of the Civil Rights Act. Increasing white support for the civil rights movement was evident in the sit-ins, the Montgomery bus boycott and the Freedom Rides. Indeed, 6 out of 13 of the original 'freedom riders' were white, and the leadership of the SCLC was multi-racial. The popularity of radical measures with whites was important for the passing of the Civil Rights Act because Kennedy's administration lacked a popular mandate and Kennedy was unwilling to take bold steps which did not enjoy public support.

The media were also influential in winning public support for the Act. Domestic and world audiences were shocked by broadcasts of Bull Connor's violence towards protesters in Birmingham in 1963. The media also showed the dignity of black protesters who remained non-violent in the face of extreme provocation. Additionally, in 1963, US magazines such as the *Wall Street Journal*, *Newsweek* and *Life Magazine* all ran articles supporting racial integration. The media's role is significant because it increased the pressure for change from both within and outside the United States.

e This paragraph has a strong explanatory focus. Importantly, the examples it uses to support its comment about the media are specific and indicate a range of knowledge beyond the obvious reference to Birmingham.

The March on Washington in 1963 demonstrated the importance of unity, popular support and the media as causes of the Civil Rights Act. Nearly a quarter of a million people of all races, and representing the major civil rights organisations, walked to the Lincoln Memorial campaigning for 'jobs and freedom'. The march gained a lot of media attention and was a catalyst for change because it proved to Kennedy that he could not afford to ignore popular pressure for change.

> The first sentence of this paragraph makes a new point and at the same time shows how it links to the previous three points. This is integration and suggests that the candidate is heading towards level 5. Moreover, the final sentence links the March on Washington to the presidents, which is the focus of the next paragraph.

Presidential support for the Act was another reason for the Act's success. Martin Luther King's support of Kennedy in 1960 was an important factor in Kennedy's election. Therefore, King had some influence on the Kennedy administration which he used to persuade Kennedy to back the bill. Kennedy's death in 1963 was also significant as it created much public sympathy for his civil rights agenda. Johnson, a supporter of the Act, skilfully used the impetus created by Kennedy's death to persuade Congress to pass the bill. Presidential support was therefore essential to the passing of the Civil Rights Act because without it Congress would never have accepted the bill.

The most significant factor that explains the passing of the Civil Rights Act was the March on Washington. This demonstrated the unity of the civil rights movement as King, members of SNCC and CORE, and the leader of the NAACP, Roy Wilkins, threw their weight behind the protest. The march also gained considerable media attention, moving the public further behind the bill. Finally, the march forced the Kennedy administration to publicly support the Act. In so doing, it brought together important individuals such as King and Kennedy, without whom success would have been impossible.

> The conclusion shows once again how the different factors relate. Moreover, it draws conclusions about the relative importance of the different factors discussed. In this sense, it is more than a simple summary.

> **This is a comprehensive, detailed and focused answer, achieving a high level 5 mark by virtue of a thorough explanation of how the different factors interlink and some consideration of relative importance.**

Level 5: 29/30

■ ▓ ▓

C-grade answer

In 1964 the much needed Civil Rights Act was passed. The Act was much needed as black people were very unequal in America at the time. The Act banned segregation in all public places and set up a department to make sure that black people had equal opportunities in their jobs.

5

question

There is one main reason for the Act, and that was President Lyndon B. Johnson who became president after Kennedy was shot. Kennedy was shot in 1963, stopping him from passing the Civil Rights Act.

e The candidate states that there is only one reason for the passing of the Civil Rights Act. Clearly this is a simplistic view of events.

Although it was sad that Kennedy was shot, Johnson was able to pass the Act because he said that it was what Kennedy would have wanted. Johnson made Kennedy's funeral very symbolic because he organised for two black people from the army and navy to carry Kennedy's coffin. This made people support the Act and made it easier to pass.

Johnson also managed to get some Republicans to support the Act. When the bill was passed, 152 Democrats supported it and 138 Republicans supported it. Only 130 politicians were against it. This shows how important Johnson and cross-party support was as a cause of the Civil Rights Act.

e Here the candidate has used some specific supporting examples which ensures that the development is secure.

Johnson was very persuasive and gave lots of speeches in favour of the Act. He also got Truman, Eisenhower and Hoover (who had been presidents before Johnson) to support the Act. His speeches were very important as without them the Act would not have been passed.

Johnson really cared for black Americans. He had a vision of a 'Great Society' in which African Americans and whites would be equal. Johnson's 'Great Society' wanted to go further than FDR's New Deal and end poverty once and for all in the USA. It also wanted to give equality of opportunity to all Americans, even African Americans. This vision was an important cause for the Act to be passed as it meant that Johnson was committed to the idea of black and white equality and so was prepared to fight for it even when people opposed him. This is different to Eisenhower's reaction when his Civil Rights Act was criticised — he backed down because he didn't really believe in it.

e Although the expression is fairly simplistic, the candidate has made a relevant point, developed it with some accurate examples and explained how Johnson's ideology led to the passing of the Act. This takes the answer to the bottom of level 3.

There were other factors that might have helped the Civil Rights Act. They were the civil rights campaigns like Little Rock. The March on Washington is a particularly important example. Martin Luther King himself is another important factor.

The central weakness of this answer is its focus on Johnson. Johnson was clearly important, but he was not the only cause of the Act. Although other factors are mentioned in the conclusion, they are entirely undeveloped. Despite this weakness the answer is awarded high level 3 due to its developed and focused explanation of Johnson's ideology, some evidence of specific knowledge (for example, the number of senators who voted for the Act), some weak explanatory links and its sustained focus.

Level 3: 17/30

PHILIP ALLAN
UPDATES

Intensive Revision Weekends

Biology
Business Studies (AQA)
Chemistry
Economics
French
German
Law (AQA or OCR)

Mathematics
Physics (Edexcel)
Politics
Psychology (AQA (A))
Religious Studies
Sociology
Spanish

- Intensive 2-day revision courses with expert tutors, including senior examiners
- Guaranteed to improve exam technique and build confidence
- Develops AS and A2 key skills
- Tests understanding of core topics
- Invaluable summary notes provided
- Ideal Central London location

Contact us today for further information: tel: 01706 831002 fax: 01706 830011
e-mail: sales@philipallanupdates.co.uk

Philip Allan Updates
Suite 16, Hardmans Business Centre, Rossendale, Lancashire BB4 6HH